A WORLD OF DUMPLINGS

Filled Dumplings, Pockets, and Little Pies from around the Globe

Brian Yarvin

with photographs by the author

A WORLD OF DUMPLINGS

Filled Dumplings, Pockets, and Little Pies from around the Globe

Brian Yarvin

with photographs by the author

The Countryman Press
Woodstock, Vermont

WE WELCOME YOUR COMMENTS AND SUGGESTIONS.
Please contact Editor, The Countryman Press, P.O. Box 748, Woodstock, Vermont 05091,
or e-mail countrymanpress@wwnorton.com.

Library of Congress Cataloging-in-Publication Data
Yarvin, Brian.
  A world of dumplings : filled dumplings, pockets, and little pies from around the globe / Brian Yarvin.
    p. cm.
  Includes index.
  ISBN 978-0-88150-720-1 (alk. paper)
  1. Stuffed foods (Cookery) I. Title.

  TX836.Y37 2007
  641.8--dc22

                2007017181

BOOK DESIGN AND COMPOSITION by Michelle Farinella Design
COVER AND INTERIOR PHOTOGRAPHS by the author

PUBLISHED BY The Countryman Press, P.O. Box 748, Woodstock, VT 05091

DISTRIBUTED BY W. W. Norton & Company, Inc., 500 Fifth Avenue, New York, NY 10110

Printed in China by R.R. Donnelley

10 9 8 7 6 5 4 3 2 1

DEDICATION

To my wife, Maria Grazia Asselle—
a dumpling fan if there ever was one

ACKNOWLEDGMENTS

So many people pitched in to make this book happen that it's hard for me to show my gratitude adequately. First and foremost, I'd like to thank my wife, Maria Asselle, who had dumplings for dinner on nights when she dreamed of something else far more often then I care to admit. At the Countryman Press, Kermit Hummel and Jennifer Thompson displayed an amazing ability to put up with the sorts of questions and issues that a project like this presents. I hope we're still on speaking terms.

I also offer special thanks to the chefs whose dishes gave me a benchmark to reach for. Some, like Yamini Joshi, Jessica Avent, Jim Weaver, and James Griffiths, spoke to me at length, while others—because of time and language barriers—could respond with only a smile or a nod. No matter . . . every lesson learned was important. Thanks to Arnie Chapman, the Association of Independent Competitive Eaters, and their sponsor, Caribbean Food Delights, for giving me red-carpet treatment during that amazing patty-eating competition. It was an unforgettable experience.

And finally, I must extend my gratitude to those people—a mix of chefs, home cooks, and actors—who allowed me to photograph them cooking and eating: Maya Anandan, Michael Anstendig, Katerina Apostolico, Kenisha Burgess, Tylil Burgess, Caitlin Capitanio, Wayne Chang, Kathy Chen, Salam Dahbour, Sherry Hwang, Yinzhen Lu, Nancy Malleo, Amanda Rising, Trevor Schneider, Stacey J. Sheng, and William L. Sheng.

CONTENTS

III. CENTRAL ASIA AND THE MIDDLE EAST 100

VI. THE AMERICAS 226

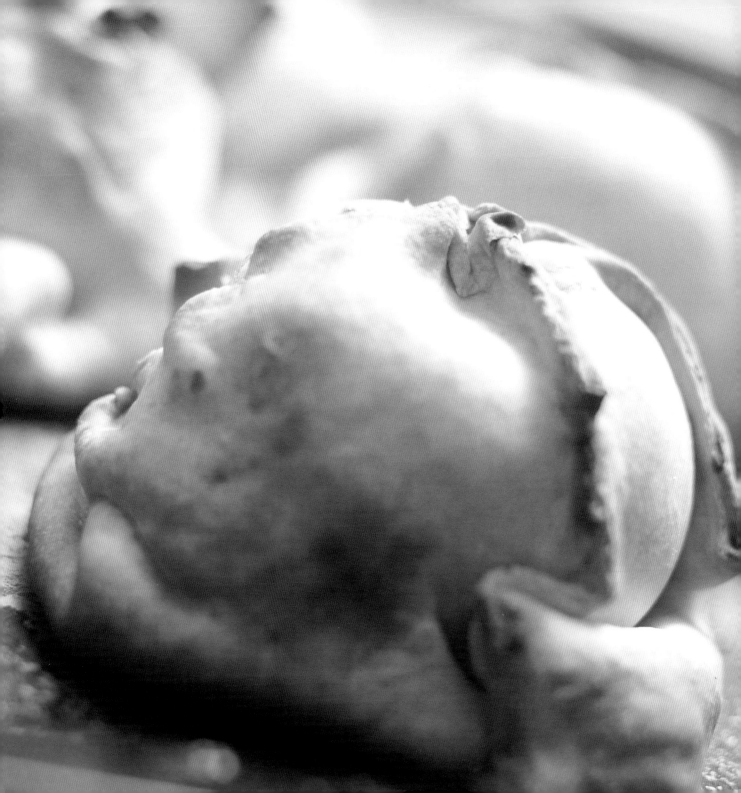

INTRODUCTION

At lunchtime in Cornwall, England, you'll see people eating a local specialty:

a sheet of dough wrapped around meat and vegetables to form a sort of self-contained meal.

Thousands of miles away in South America, crowds gather around a vendor offering a snack:

a bit of meat and vegetable wrapped with a piece of dough. In China, Italy, Japan, Poland,

Turkey, and a host of other countries, this scene is repeated every day. The dumpling—the

most universal of all foods—is everywhere.

Dumplings are a common thread in cuisines throughout the world, similar in basic concept but often wildly different in the details. The ones from Cornwall—they're known as "pasties"—are bigger than a man's fist and have a flaky crust, while the *pelmini* of Eastern Europe are smaller than a fingernail. Vietnamese spring rolls have a wrapping so delicate it's almost transparent, and Polish pierogi have a skin that's thick, almost chewy, and redolent of sour cream.

What is it that unites these far-flung foods? Is it more than just a rough description? And how do these common items show their differences? In this book, we will explore what makes pierogi Polish and *mandu* Korean. We'll find out how *gyoza* differ from *shu mai,* and why all of them are different than ravioli.

You could travel the world in search of the essential dumpling, but there's really no need. Modern America provides countless opportunities to sample every variety imaginable: Cornish pasties in your local pub, shu mai at the Chinese restaurant, ravioli from a neighborhood Italian deli, and pierogi at a church supper. Taken as a category, dumplings transcend all barriers. You can grab them at a snack bar or spend an afternoon making them with friends and family. There's a bit of joy inside each one.

THE BASICS

A World of Definitions—Or Just What *Is* a Filled Dumpling, Anyway?

One of the first questions that people ask me is: "Just what is a filled dumpling, anyway?" Followed by, "What makes it filled?" The *Merriam-Webster Online Dictionary* defines "dumpling" as "(a) a small mass of leavened dough cooked by boiling or steaming" or "(b) a usually baked dessert of fruit wrapped in dough." This sounded pretty good to me, although the "leavened" part means that pierogi, ravioli, and most of the Chinese section wouldn't qualify.

I sought out another definition, this time from *The Food Lover's Companion*, second edition, by Sharon Tyler Herbst: "Savory dumplings are small or large mounds of dough that are usually dropped into a liquid mixture (such as soup or stew) and cooked until done. Some are stuffed with meat or cheese mixtures. Dessert dumplings most often consist of a fruit mixture encased in a sweet pastry dough and baked. They're usually served with a sauce. Some sweet dumplings are poached in a sweet sauce and served with cream." I liked this definition a lot—especially the part about poaching in a sweet sauce—but it still left out ones that were steamed, boiled in water, baked, or fried. In other words, almost every dumpling that I knew.

All this called for a new definition, one that would allow for all sorts of foods commonly known as "dumplings" to be included. So . . . just what *is* a dumpling? More specifically, a filled dumpling? How about: a food item that consists of a dough-based outer wrapper with a distinct, separate filling inside.

. . . Wrapped in Dough

One thing that all the recipes in this book have in common is dough. There may be every sort of filling, but there's always that stuff on the outside. So for that reason, we'll begin with a few

words about dough making. There's something very gratifying about it. Maybe it's the kneading with its vigorous action or perhaps the primal-ness; after all, flour-water doughs are among the earliest known cooked foods.

Viewed collectively, the doughs here have an astounding range of ingredients; everything from mashed potatoes to curry powder can find its way into a recipe. But all share wheat flour and water.

Just what does wheat flour do? Besides being a great source of carbs, it contains a specific kind of protein that's pretty much the only source of gluten that gives dough its texture. You can do lots with other grain flours, but they'll never knead into the sort of dough that wheat will. Aside from the gluten, this is where water comes in, too.

Gluten is a mixture of wheat protein and water with a unique feature: When kneaded, it has elasticity and can stretch and form the distinctive consistency that we prize in breads, cakes, and pastas. The recipes here take advantage of this in two ways. Yeast-raised doughs become lighter with their distinctive body, and pastas become chewier and acquire that "al dente" character.

So when you're kneading and wondering why, it's because that effort you put in builds the flavors that homemade dumpling wrappers offer. Not all recipes have long kneading times; the ones closest to pie doughs are kneaded only for a minute or so. That way they build up enough gluten to hold the dumpling together but not enough to make it tough.

Pasta Machine 101

I've always thought of pasta machines as being something that's as Italian as could be—that is, until I took a pierogi-making class a few years ago. There, the noted author and cooking teacher Daniel Rosati used a pasta machine for those very same Eastern European dumplings. Since then, I've tried it with many other recipes, and it really makes life easier.

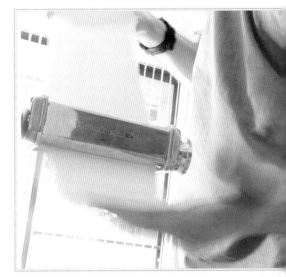

Typical pasta machines are fairly simple; they have two steel rollers, a knob that allows the space between the rollers to be adjusted, and a hand crank or motor to turn them. Using one is as simple as passing the dough between the rollers while they're turning, but there are a few things to think about.

First of all, the machine makes long strips of dough, no matter what shape they start out as, so you'll have to have a flat, floured surface to lay them down on. Second, the trip between those steel rollers is a very special type of kneading. Because of wheat's gluten-based elasticity, the dough will bounce back somewhat after its trip, so you'll have to make several repeat passes to get the dough right. You'll know it's there when its surface is smooth and even, and it's no longer breaking or forming odd shapes.

So how exactly do you use a pasta machine? Begin with a batch of your favorite dough. Cut off about one-third of it, and use the palm of your hand to flatten it out. Set the machine to its widest thickness, usually "1."

Feed the dough through the rollers; at first it might crumble, but after three or four repetitions, the kneading process gets going. Change the machine's setting, narrow the gap between the rollers one notch (usually to "2"), and put the dough through a few more times. Continue the pattern of narrowing the rollers and passing the dough through until you have a sheet of dough the thickness you need— almost always a "4" or "5" for the recipes in this book. When the sheets of dough are ready, place them between layers of parchment paper until you're going to use them. That way they won't dry out.

Using (or Not) That Food Processor and Buying (or Not) a Knife

When I began to get serious about dumplings a few years ago, the first thing I did was buy a large, professional-looking food processor with a suitably French name and maybe two or three thousand accessory plates and blades. I was really proud!

Some 20 or 30 fillings later, it seemed that my new toy was a bit too much. Often it would turn everything into a banal paste in a second or two, and other times the ingredients would just spin in circles at an amazing rate of speed.

What did I really need?

A good knife, a clean cutting board, and a standard home-kitchen food processor. Some people would add "a quiet moment to use them," but I learned that my own reality was almost exactly the opposite of this. All I needed to do to create a quiet moment was to pull out the knife and cutting board and start chopping. I always felt better afterward.

I went though a similar thing with knives; buying "name-brand" blades with high prices and yelling at my wife when she put them in the dishwasher. A visit to Chef Jim Weaver at Tre Piani Restaurant (see page 198) cured me. They use simple, commercial knives that are easily washed and resharpened. The food they create with their no-brand knives is dazzling. I couldn't imagine anybody dining there and then saying, "The meal would have been sublime if only they'd used a better knife."

Good knife skills are helpful, but don't let inexperience stop you from trying these recipes. If you feel the need, most cooking schools have knife-skills classes that can improve the abilities of the average home cook by a couple of thousand percent in an afternoon. Even so, maybe you and I can't chop like those guys on TV, but our food can still be delicious.

Parchment Paper

Whenever I mention this essential item, people always seem to think I'm talking about ancient documents—or at least something that looks like it's old. But parchment paper is nothing of the sort. Used to make sure that sticky foods don't adhere to cooking and storage surfaces, it's an essential in the dumpling maker's kitchen.

If you're filling and folding dumplings and then setting them aside before cooking or freezing, putting them on parchment paper is a good way to make sure that they don't stick to whatever it is you put them on. Whether you're storing them overnight in the fridge or even in the freezer, you won't be leaving bits and pieces of wrapper dough on your plates, platters, and baking sheets.

Parchment paper is a stealth product. Employees of stores that sell carloads of the stuff often don't know they have it. So you not only have to ask, but you also have to look carefully. These days the best place to find it is right by the foils and plastic wraps in the supermarket. Fancy kitchen-supply stores will often have a fancier product—perhaps organic or unbleached— but I haven't found the need.

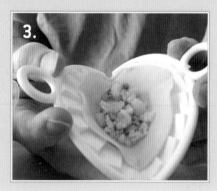

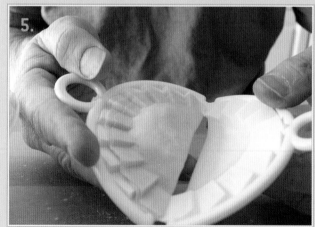

The Half-Moon Fold and the Dumpling Press

There are some folds that look hard (think "Shanghai-Style Soup Dumplings," page 58, with their 16 pinches), and others that initially just baffled me—samosas come to mind here. But most of the recipes in this book don't require this sort of challenge. Instead, they use what I call the half-moon fold. Just a disk of dough folded in half and sealed at the edges.

This technique is the same across the globe, from Japan to Jamaica, and you'll often find a tool to help; I've dubbed it the dumpling press. These clam-shaped gizmos open up to provide a place where you can put a circle of wrapper dough and a bit of filling. You then fold them in half along the hinge, where the pressure forms a perfect dumpling and a good seal.

Dumpling presses come in all different sizes, depending on where in the world you are. In Cornwall, England, they're big enough to hold a ball of filling the size of an orange (see "Local Pubs: Something British on the Menu," page 221), and in Italy, there are ones that leave you with a dumpling smaller than some coins. In the U.S. you can easily find them in Asian housewares stores. But Eastern European and Italian shops will occasionally have them, too. Don't look in the fancy places just yet, though, since nobody's manufacturing a stainless steel and rosewood model—but maybe soon. . . .

Deep Frying

The way some people talk about deep frying, you'd think it took more skill than watchmaking. And to hear some others, a person could conclude that it's more dangerous than smoking in bed. Most of us don't usually deep fry at home, and the few that do it almost always have dedicated deep-fryers.

So how about those people who want to fry up a batch of dumplings every now and then?

Gather together a few things—a heavy four-quart pot, a wire-basket spoon or slotted spoon, the sort of thermometer that clips to the edge of the pot—and go to it. You can easily find these items in the housewares section of a good Asian or Latin American supermarket. Otherwise, a restaurant supplier will have what you need.

Oil? The deep-fried recipes in this book were tested with peanut oil. It's inexpensive, and the only off-flavor I ever detect is that of peanuts. Canola and other vegetable oils seem perfect, too, but sadly, even some premium products can develop strange tastes if they're overheated.

Around the Mediterranean, you'll find cooks using low-grade olive oil (which is cheap in that corner of the world), but it's easy to scorch and smoke. Don't be tempted to try extra virgin olive oil, either; it becomes tasteless at this temperature and does nothing for the food. Save it for pan frying, salads, and the many other uses in which it excels.

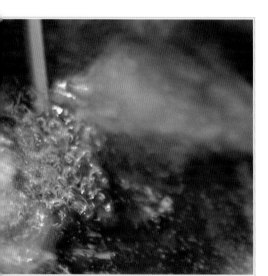

If you ever get the chance, frying with top-quality lard delivers flavors and textures that are meaty, crunchy, and utterly fantastic. Rendering instructions are on page 269, but be forewarned: You'll need at least 15 pounds of leaf lard or pork belly to make three quarts ready for the pot.

Finally, if you must skimp, just fry in a smaller pot. Yamini, the samosa and kachori master profiled on page 87, used only a quart of oil at a time. As long as she fried just a few pieces in a batch, things were great.

Steaming

For some of us, steaming is the blah cooking technique of health-food fanatics. The very thought of "steamed veggies"— and it's always "veggies," never "vegetables"—is completely off-putting. Steaming is a worthy technique, though; it has a way of making the flavor of the filling blend with the wrapper dough to create a single, delicious mass.

I've found that the best way to steam is in circular bamboo trays sold for the purpose. You line them with a layer of Napa cabbage (a.k.a. Chinese cabbage), and place the uncooked dumplings on top. Then take a large pot, add about a half inch of water, put the steamer baskets inside, and cover. Cook over medium heat for the time called for in the recipe.

And I might as well let you in on a personal secret: After finishing a couple of baskets of dumplings, I'll gather up the cabbage leaves at the bottom and eat them. My wife, who thinks I'm doing this because I have an odd obsession with green vegetables, overlooks hers without a second thought. She doesn't know that the cabbage is infused with dumpling flavor and is often as good as the dumplings themselves.

Freezing

There seem to be two secrets to freezing dumplings: Don't use ingredients that were frozen before without cooking them first, and make sure your freezer is as cold as it should be. Once you've established those two basics, you're ready to get going. You'll need a cookie sheet, enough parchment paper to cover it, and sufficient plastic freezer bags to hold your production.

Lay the sheet of parchment paper on top of the cookie sheet, and on it place the dumplings you want to freeze—filled, folded, and uncooked—making sure that none touch each other. Put the cookie sheet in the freezer, and leave it undisturbed for at least three hours. When the dumplings are frozen solid (and not before!), put them in plastic bag's, then return them to the freezer.

Don't forget to clearly mark the bag's with their contents and the date. I promise you that no matter how excited you are the day they're made, you'll forget what's in the bags a few months later.

Some Final Cooking Tips

An Optional Egg Wash

Walk into a shop where almost any of the baked items in this book are served, and you'll often see products glistening as if they were waxed. Eat the same thing in a private home, and it will look like a plain crust of bread. What's the difference? To get that shine, the dough is brushed with beaten egg just before popping it in the oven. That's called an "egg wash."

Most home cooks—myself including—will leave out the egg wash. Why? More egg equals more cholesterol plus more fat. So if you want your baked dumplings to sport the sort of commercial shine you were hoping to duplicate, a quick brushing with beaten egg will do the trick. And if you're worried about how healthy this is, here's a tip: Use one of those egg substitute products. They'll get your crusts glowing just as well as the real thing.

Make the Sacrifice

How can you tell when the meat fillings in dumplings are done? Often enough, your timer alone will give you the information you need, but sometimes you just have to peek inside. No dumpling in this book is intended to have its meat served rare. So when you figure they're done, test one by removing it from the pot and cutting it open. There should be no visible pink. If it's cooked through, eat the halves and don't tell anybody. If it's still a bit underdone, you'll have to trash it—a sacrifice for a good cause—and cook the rest a bit longer.

ASIA

A Visit to Dumpling Central: Flushing, Queens

"Dumplings? Have you gone to Flushing yet?"

Whenever any New York City food fanatics heard about my quest for dumplings, they told me about Flushing. This semi-suburban neighborhood—home to Shea Stadium and LaGuardia Airport—is deep in the borough of Queens. It's the city's largest settlement of Asian immigrants and a magnet for those who seek uncompromising regional cuisines.

It all started in the early seventies, when Chinatown residents were looking beyond their lower Manhattan neighborhood for other places to settle. They couldn't have found a better spot. There was public transit, good housing, a retail center, and even some industrial space. Word spread quickly, and by the middle of the eighties, Koreans, Malaysians, and Indians had joined them and made the place one of the largest Asian immigrant communities in the eastern United States.

There are pockets of Chinese culture all over the country, of course, and the sort of authentic experience that was only available in a few major cities three decades ago is now fairly widespread. But as anybody who has visited the Far East knows, a whole category of foods is missing. Not what you get in a nice restaurant or even in a friend's home, but what local people buy at vendors, snack bars, and small shops: "street food"—dumplings, or dim sum. If you want Chinese street food in the New York area, Flushing is where you have to head.

I got off the train at Main Street, Flushing's subway station, and I wanted to get some dumplings. I had no trouble at all. From chic cafés to sidewalk stands, they're sold by vendors, at small plain snack shops, and in fancy dim sum restaurants. Everywhere I went, I saw people meeting for a bite in the same way that they might get together for a drink in other parts of the city.

I joined the crowd that had gathered at the Railway Host Shops on Main Street, directly under the Long Island Railroad station. Behind a glass window was a wok of steamed yeast-bread buns filled with spiced pork. They were four for a dollar, and customers started eating them before they even left the cashier. If there is a "signature" dumpling here, it's that stuffed bread. I sat down and ate a batch across the street on the library steps.

The little White Bear Ice Cream Shop on Prince Street between 40th and Roosevelt is a hidden treasure. Really a tiny dumpling-and-noodle place, it has plates of spicy wontons and bowls of soups. The handful of seats are always occupied, but if you wait just a moment or two, one will open up. When I finally got my chance, the woman behind the counter cheerfully

greeted me in Chinese, and by pointing, I ordered what everybody else seemed to be eating: wontons with chili sauce (my recipe is on page 67). They came drenched in hot oil and sprinkled with toasted sesame seeds and chopped pickled radish. It turned out that the minimum order was 12, but so what? After all I'd eaten that afternoon, why not more dumplings?

Afterward, on the number 7 train, I noticed how many of my fellow passengers had boarded with food—dumplings, of course! I tried to guess where they came from, but couldn't. I had devoured almost 40, but hadn't even scratched the surface of possible eateries.

Japanese Steamed Sweet Bean Paste Bun's (Goma-anko Manju)

Japanese Fried Dumplings (Gyoza)

Makes 25 dumplings

Gyoza are classic Japanese dumplings filled with pork and cabbage. You'll find similar recipes all though Asia, but these, with sugar and a half-moon shape, have a Japanese touch.

FILLING

1 cup finely chopped napa cabbage

2 tablespoons finely chopped scallions

1 pound ground pork

1 tablespoon sesame oil

1 tablespoon sugar

2 tablespoons soy sauce

2 cloves garlic, finely minced

1 tablespoon grated fresh ginger

WRAPPERS

"Chinese Wheat-Flour Dumpling
            Wrappers," page 48

Vegetable oil for frying

1. To make the filling, combine the cabbage, scallions, ground pork, sesame oil, sugar, soy sauce, garlic, and ginger in a bowl. Using your hands or a potato masher, mix the ingredients together thoroughly, making sure that they are well combined and evenly distributed.

2. Spoon a teaspoon of filling in the center of a round dumpling wrapper, fold the disk in half, and pinch it shut. This is the classic half-moon shape and fold (see page 25). If you use commercial wrappers, you'll need to wet the edges with water.

3. Heat the oil (1/8 inch deep is fine) in a nonstick frying pan over medium heat. Fry the gyoza in small batches, turning them over frequently. Make sure the meat filling is cooked all the way through (see "Make the Sacrifice," page 31); there should be no sign of pink in the middle, the wrappers should be crisp golden-brown, and the juices should run clear. Drain on paper towels before serving.

Gyoza Dipping Sauce

Makes 1/2 cup

Mix the soy sauce, sugar, teriyaki sauce, scallions, and sesame oil together in a small bowl. Let stand for at least 15 minutes before serving so that the flavors can combine properly.

1 teaspoon soy sauce

1 tablespoon brown sugar

3 tablespoons teriyaki sauce

1 tablespoon finely chopped scallions

2 tablespoons sesame oil

Japanese Steamed Sweet Bean Paste Buns (Goma-anko Manju)

Makes 10 dumplings

This sweet Japanese dumpling makes a great snack—or maybe even a dessert for an all-dumpling meal.

FILLING

1 cup anko (sweet azuki bean paste)

3 tablespoons water

2 tablespoons black sesame seeds, toasted (see note)

NOTE: To toast sesame seeds, preheat your oven to 325 degrees, spread the seeds on a baking sheet, and bake for 10 minutes or until they are brown at the edges.

WRAPPERS

2 tablespoons sugar

1/2 cup warm water

2 cups cake flour

1/2 teaspoon baking powder

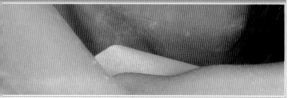

1. To make the filling, warm the bean paste in a saucepan over low heat. Mix in the water and toasted sesame seeds. Remove from the heat, set aside, and let cool to room temperature.

2. To make the wrappers, mix the sugar with the warm water, and stir until dissolved. In a medium bowl, combine the flour and baking powder, and then add the sugar water, stirring thoroughly. Knead for 3 to 5 minutes or until it becomes a dough.

3. Slice the dough into pieces about 3/4 inch long, and roll each piece into a ball. Cover with parchment paper to prevent them from drying out. On a floured work surface, roll out each ball into a thin disk about 4 inches in diameter (use a cookie cutter or small bowl as a template). A piece of parchment paper between the dough and the rolling pin will make things a bit easier.

4. To fill the wrappers, spoon a teaspoon of filling into the center of each disk, pinch the edges together until you have a half-ball shape, seal the remaining hole at the top, and flip upside-down so that the bun appears smooth. For a better look, see the step-by-step photos for "Steamed Shiitake and Mustard Green Buns" on page 39. The technique is exactly the same.

5. Steam for 10 minutes, and serve warm.

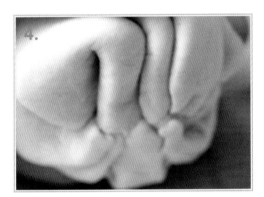

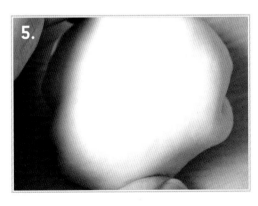

Beef Ma

Korean Dumplings (Mandu)

With a traditional half-moon shape and uniquely local fillings like kimchi, these dumplings are a great introduction to Korean ingredients and methods.

Korean Dumpling (Mandu) Wrappers

Makes 50 wrappers

Korean dumpling wrappers are similar to the basic Chinese flour-and-water recipe on page 48, but they have a twist: added salt and oil. This gives them a bit of texture and makes them much easier to handle.

3 cups all-purpose flour

2 tablespoons peanut oil

1 teaspoon salt

1 cup boiling water

1. Put the flour, oil, and salt in a large bowl, and stir in the boiling water. Use a wooden spoon to get the mixture well blended. If the dough is dry and cracking, add more water 1 tablespoon at a time until it's moist and springy; if the dough is too sticky, add more flour 1 tablespoon at a time until it's smooth. After the mixture cools a bit, knead it with your hands for about 7 minutes or until a poke with a finger causes it to bounce back like a soft pillow. Then cover the dough in plastic wrap and refrigerate for about 30 minutes.

2. To make the dumpling wrappers, slice the dough into pieces about 3/4 inch long, and roll each piece into a ball. On a floured work surface, roll out each ball into a thin disk about 4 inches in diameter. A piece of parchment paper between the dough and the rolling pin will make things a bit easier.

3. Fill with "Spicy Cabbage and Chicken" (page 43) or "Fried Beef, Vegetable, and Tofu" (page 45).

Spicy Cabbage and Chicken Dumplings
Makes 35 dumplings

Most dumplings are mild and soothing, but these get their spice from that most unique of Korean ingredients, kimchi. Especially appreciated by chili heads, it has an extra-large dose of fire. If you haven't eaten kimchi before, you're in for a surprise, a kick, a thrill, or maybe a shock.

1. To make the filling, combine the cabbage, scallions, and kimchi in a colander, and make sure they are well drained. Mix these vegetables with the ground chicken, rice wine, sesame oil, salt, and pepper in a large bowl. If you use your hands, make sure you wear rubber or vinyl food-handling gloves; the chili in the kimchi can burn!

2. Fill the dumplings using the traditional "Half-Moon Method" (see page 25): Spoon a teaspoon of filling into the center of a round dumpling wrapper, fold the disk in half, and pinch it shut. If you use commercial skins, you'll need to wet the edges with water.

3. Bring the salted water to a boil in a large pot. Add the filled dumplings to the boiling water using a slotted spoon or wire basket, return to a boil, then reduce to a simmer. Cook for 6 minutes or until the meat is completely done, stirring every now and then to make sure that they don't stick to the pot but not so much that they burst.

4. Gently remove the dumplings using the same utensil you used to put them in. Drain and then serve with dipping sauce.

FILLING

1 cup chopped napa cabbage

2 tablespoons finely chopped scallions

1 cup finely chopped whole-cabbage kimchi

1 pound ground chicken

2 tablespoons Chinese rice wine

1 tablespoon sesame oil

1/2 teaspoon salt

1/2 teaspoon ground white pepper

WRAPPERS

"Korean Dumpling Wrappers," page 42

6 quarts salted water

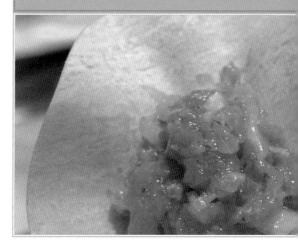

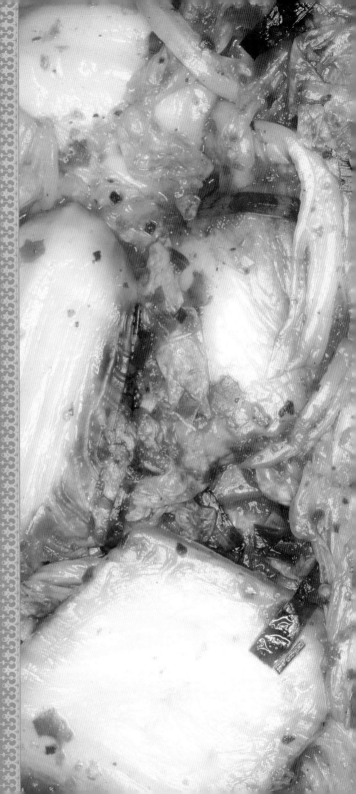

Just What Is "Kimchi"?

Kimchi are Korean pickled vegetables. They're eaten either as a side dish or ingredient at almost every meal and offer a remarkable variety of flavors and textures: the heat of chilies, the crunch of radishes or cabbage, and the pungency of sugar, salt, and vinegar.

Asian stores of almost every stripe will have jars of tongbaechu kimchi (sometimes it's just called baechu kimchi), which is whole-cabbage kimchi, the key ingredient for "Spicy Cabbage and Chicken Dumplings" (see page 43). But Korean specialty stores will have a dozen or more varieties besides.

In the kimchi department of my local Korean supermarket I found jars of stuffed cucumber, young radish, green onion, and "premium oyster." Many of the same ones were also available in gallon-sized plastic bags. Smaller containers held more exotic varieties (almost always without English names), such as the souplike namak kimchi.

In Korean culture, there's really no such thing as a one-pot meal, and kimchi most often appears as part of the assortment of small dishes collectively called "panchan," which might also include cubes of tofu, slices of raw onion, and even green salad with Russian dressing. This is served before the main course and is replenished until you're ready for dessert.

Is it something you should try? Well, if you're searching for new, hot flavors, you'll be thrilled. But kimchi is always a challenge and not for the mild mannered or faint of heart.

44

Fried Beef, Vegetable, and Tofu Dumplings

Makes 50 dumplings

Fans of Korean food will find these dumplings to be a real shock; they're mild enough for a baby and don't have a trace of chili in their filling.

1. To make the filling, heat the 2 tablespoons oil in a frying pan or wok over medium heat. Add the beef, and cook and stir for about 10 minutes or until the beef is golden brown. Crumble it with a fork to make sure it stays in small pieces. Add the onion and cabbage and cook, stirring for about another 10 minutes or until the onion begins to turn golden at the edges. Mix in the bean sprouts, scallions, and mashed tofu, making sure all the ingredients are well combined and evenly distributed. Cook for about 3 minutes or until the sprouts become translucent. Transfer the meat mixture to a bowl, and add the hoisin sauce, salt, and pepper, and mix well. Drain the filling mixture in a colander, set aside, and let cool.

2. Spoon a teaspoon of filling into the center of each wrapper, fold the disk in half, and seal the edges by pinching them (see page 25). If you use premade commercial wrappers, moisten them so that they can seal properly.

3. Put the remaining 2 cups oil in a wok or heavy skillet, and heat to 350 degrees. Carefully put the dumplings in the hot oil, and fry for about 2 minutes, or until the skin is golden brown. If the oil isn't deep enough to cover the dumplings, turn them over and make sure both sides are cooked. Drain and serve with "Mandu Dipping Sauce," page 46.

FILLING

2 tablespoons peanut oil plus 2 cups for frying

1/2 pound ground beef (chuck is fine)

1/2 cup finely chopped yellow onion (about 1 small onion)

1/2 cup finely chopped napa cabbage

1/2 cup chopped bean sprouts

1/4 cup finely chopped scallions

8 ounces (2 cakes) firm tofu, drained and mashed

3 tablespoons hoisin sauce

2 teaspoons salt

1 teaspoon freshly ground black pepper

WRAPPERS

"Korean Dumpling Wrappers," page 42

NOTE: Both tofu and bean sprouts are known for their poor freezing qualities. Choose different ingredients if this is part of your plan.

Mandu Dipping Sauce

Makes 1/2 cup

Combine the soy sauce, vinegar, sugar, sesame oil, and sesame seeds in a small bowl. Let stand for 15 minutes before serving so that the flavors can combine.

1/4 cup soy sauce

3 tablespoons rice wine vinegar

1 tablespoon brown sugar

2 tablespoon sesame oil

1 tablespoon sesame seeds

A close-up of the finished "Pinched-Edge Fold"

Chinese Wheat-Flour Dumpling Wrappers

Makes 50 wrappers

Wheat-flour wrappers for Chinese dumplings are a fairly common sight in supermarkets these days. But once you taste homemade, with their richer flavor and chewy texture, you'll never use prepared ones again.

3 cups all-purpose flour plus extra flour for the work surface

1 cup boiling water

NOTE: If you're used to filling commercial wrappers, you'll find these much more supple. There's no need to wet the edges when sealing them, either.

1. Put the flour in a large bowl, and add the boiling water. Use a wooden spoon to get the mixture well blended. If the dough is dry and cracking, add more water 1 tablespoon at a time until it's moist and springy. If the dough is sticky, add more flour 1 tablespoon at a time until it's smooth. When the mixture has cooled a bit, knead it for about 7 minutes or until a poke with a finger causes it to bounce back like a soft pillow. Cover the dough in plastic wrap, and refrigerate for about 30 minutes.

2. After the dough has rested, use your thumb to poke a hole in the center. Gradually enlarge the hole until it looks like a large bagel. Using a sort of hand-over-hand technique (see photos), squeeze the dough until it forms a rope about 3/4 inch in diameter.

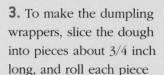

3. To make the dumpling wrappers, slice the dough into pieces about 3/4 inch long, and roll each piece into a ball. On a floured work surface, roll out the ball into a thin disk about 3 inches in diameter. A piece of parchment paper between the dough and the rolling pin will make things a bit easier.

4. Store the formed wrappers between sheets of parchment or waxed paper so that they don't dry out. If you won't be working with them within a few minutes, refrigerate them.

5. Use in any recipe that calls for them.

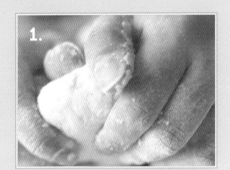

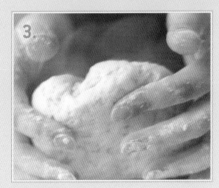

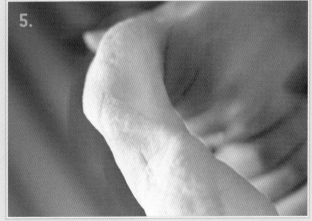

The Pinched-Edge Fold

Sit down to a dim sum meal, or just a plate of dumplings at a good Chinese restaurant, and you'll find the pinched-edge fold. Sometimes you'll just see part of the edge pinched, but with "Shanghai-Style Soup Dumplings" (see page 58) and their cousins, the edge will be pinched all the way around, forming a sort of dome.

This is a dumpling shape that most people think of as uniquely Chinese, but it pops up once more along the Silk Road. In the Republic of Georgia, a local favorite called "khinkali" (see page 116) uses the exact same technique. It vanishes from this point west, though, and while half moons are found all across the world, the pinched-edge fold never even made it to Europe.

These photos show how it's done.

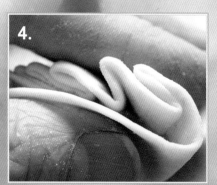

Cantonese Shrimp Dumplings

Makes 50 dumplings

These shrimp-filled dumplings are a little bit of luxury. Maybe they don't have caviar, but in the minds of many eaters, the seafood elevates them from the usual pork.

1. To make the filling, combine the shrimp, scallions, water chestnuts, egg whites, cornstarch, salt, pepper, soy sauce, and peanut oil in a food processor, and pulse until you have a coarse paste.

2. Fill the wrappers as shown in "The Half-Moon Fold and the Dumpling Press" on page 25 or "The Pinched-Edge Fold" on page 50. As always, if you use commercial wrappers, you'll need to moisten the edges to get things to stick.

3. Line your steamer basket with a single layer of napa cabbage leaves, and steam the dumplings over medium heat for 8 minutes or until the egg white is completely cooked. If you're using the stackable bamboo steamer inserts, rotate them after 4 minutes so that each layer gets a chance to be close to the heat.

4. Serve with "Soy-Vinegar Dipping Sauce," page 70.

Variation

Instead of combining the ingredients in a food processor, chop them finely with a knife. The results aren't better or worse, but the taste is quite different for something with the same ingredients.

FILLING

1 pound raw shrimp, shelled and deveined

3 scallions

6 water chestnuts

2 egg whites

1 1/2 teaspoons cornstarch

1 teaspoon salt

1/2 teaspoon ground white pepper

1 tablespoon soy sauce

1 tablespoon peanut oil

WRAPPERS

"Chinese Wheat-Flour Dumpling Wrappers,"
     page 48

Napa cabbage leaves for the steamer basket

A Bit of Color

At a great dim sum meal, the wide variety of dumpling colors is part of the entertainment. Yes, you can bet that some of the bigger places just use food dyes, but there is also a tradition of adding natural ingredients that change both shade and taste.

The two basics are spinach leaves for green and carrot for orange. Here are the recipes:

FOR GREEN

1 cup wilted or frozen chopped spinach leaves

FOR ORANGE

1 cup carrot pieces, boiled until fork tender

Combine either ingredient (but not both together!) in a blender with 1 cup of water. Puree until you have a smooth liquid. Substitute this for water in any Chinese dumpling wrapper recipe.

FOR YELLOW

Yellow is another story! This color is from curry flavoring, which requires careful matching with fillings. I find it works best with "Steamed Chinese Pork Dumplings" (see page 56) or wontons (see page 64) and is created by adding a teaspoon of curry powder to each cup of dry flour before the liquid is added.

Chinese-Style Chicken Dumplings

Makes 40 dumplings

By adding strong flavors, this dumpling avoids the blandness that too many people associate with chicken. What you get can be great steamed, pan fried, or even deep fried. And consider adding color to the wrappers (see "A Bit of Color," page 52).

1. To make the filling, combine the chicken, cabbage, garlic, scallions, ginger, cilantro, soy sauce, vinegar, oil, and pepper in a food processor, and blend into a thick paste.

2. Fill the dumplings using the traditional half-moon method (see page 25).

3. Cooking variations:

To deep fry: Heat 3 quarts of peanut oil in a heavy pot over medium or medium-high heat, and stir occasionally until it reaches 375 degrees (see "Deep-Frying" page 25). Gently lower the dumplings into the oil using a slotted spoon or wire basket made for this purpose. Cook until the dumplings are golden brown. Remove from the oil using the same utensil you used to put them in. Drain on paper towels before serving.

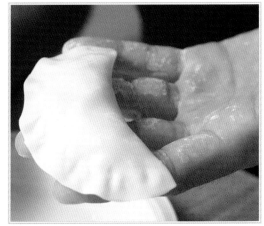

FILLING

1 1/2 pounds ground chicken

1 cup chopped napa cabbage (about 3 ounces)

4 cloves garlic

2 tablespoons minced scallions

1 tablespoon peeled fresh ginger

1 cup cilantro leaves

2 tablespoons soy sauce

1 tablespoon black vinegar

1 tablespoon sesame oil

1 teaspoon ground white pepper

WRAPPERS

"Chinese Wheat-Flour Dumpling Wrappers," page 48 (see note)

To pan fry: Heat 2 tablespoons peanut oil in a nonstick frying pan over medium heat. Fry the dumplings in small batches, turning them over frequently. Make sure the meat filling is thoroughly cooked with no sign of pink in the middle (see "Make the Sacrifice," page 31). The wrappers should be a crisp golden-brown, and the juices should run clear. Drain or not, as you prefer.

To steam: Line your steamer basket with a single layer of napa cabbage leaves, and steam the dumplings over high heat for about 15 minutes or until the meat is completely cooked (again, see "Make the Sacrifice"). If you're using the stackable bamboo steamer inserts, rotate them every 5 minutes so that each layer gets a chance to be close to the heat. Serve immediately.

Serve with "Soy-Vinegar Dipping Sauce," page 70.

Chinese Cabbage and Mushroom Dumplings

Makes 40 dumplings

Try these vegetable dumplings when you need a refreshing change from meat-filled recipes. They're also great for vegetarians.

NOTE: You'll need to use fresh wrappers for this dish; commercial ones won't bind together tightly enough to hold this loose filling.

1. To make the filling, combine the carrot, mushrooms, scallions, chopped cabbage, soy sauce, garlic, ginger, pepper, and sugar in a large bowl, and mix thoroughly.

2. Fill the dumplings using the "Pinched Half-Moon Method" (see page 25).

3. Line your steamer basket with a single layer of napa cabbage leaves, and steam the dumplings over high heat for 8 minutes or until the mushroom's are completely cooked. If you're using the stackable bamboo steamer inserts, rotate them every 4 minutes so that each layer gets a chance to be close to the heat.

4. Serve with "Soy-Vinegar Dipping Sauce," page 70.

Variation
For an interesting contrast, try the "Steamed Shiitake and Mustard Green Buns" (see page 62) or "Cabbage and Mushroom Pierogi" (see page 158) with really similar ingredients and techniques but a very different end result.

FILLING

1 small carrot, finely chopped

2 cups finely chopped fresh shiitake mushroom caps (about 6 ounces)

5 scallions, finely chopped

2 cups finely chopped napa cabbage plus extra cabbage leaves for the steamer basket

1 tablespoon soy sauce

2 garlic cloves, finely chopped

1/2 teaspoon ground white pepper

1/2 teaspoon sugar

WRAPPERS

"Chinese Wheat-Flour Dumpling Wrappers," page 48 (see note)

Steamed Chinese Pork Dumplings (Shu Mai)

Makes 25 dumplings

This is one of the basics—that simple steamed dumpling you see in every dim sum restaurant and appetizer menu. Chinese wheat-flour dumpling wrappers are classic.

FILLING

1 pound ground pork

1 tablespoon minced scallions

1 cup minced bean sprouts (about 4 ounces)

2 teaspoons minced fresh ginger

1/2 cup shredded carrot

1 tablespoon soy sauce

1 tablespoon Chinese rice wine

1/2 teaspoon salt

1 tablespoon sesame oil

1/2 teaspoon sugar

1/4 teaspoon ground white pepper

WRAPPERS

"Chinese Wheat-Flour Dumpling Wrappers," page 48

Napa cabbage leaves to line the steamer basket

1. To make the filling, combine the pork, scallions, sprouts, ginger, carrots, soy sauce, rice wine, salt, sesame oil, sugar, and pepper in large bowl, and mix thoroughly so that everything is well distributed. (I find a potato masher great for this purpose.)

2. To make the dumpling, spoon 1 teaspoon of filling into the center of the wrapper. Bring up the sides of the wrapper, and close them with pinching and folding motions.

3. Line your steamer basket with a single layer of napa cabbage leaves, and steam the dumplings over high heat for 15 minutes or until the meat is completely cooked (see "Make the Sacrifice," page 31). If you're using the stackable bamboo steamer inserts, rotate them every 5 minutes so that each layer gets a chance to be close to the heat.

4. Serve with "Soy-Vinegar Dipping Sauce," page 70.

Shanghai-Style Soup Dumplings (Xiao Long Bao)

Makes 25 dumplings

A dish? A fad? A genre? An item of cult worship? Soup dumplings are constantly talked about and frequently sought out. When I started telling people about my interest in dumplings, this was the one they invariably asked for.

To make them, you first prepare the soup, then the filling, then the wrappers. Finally, you fill the wrappers and steam them. The third step you will find on page 48. The other steps are on the following pages.

Soup for Shanghai-Style Soup Dumplings

Makes 2 cups

This recipe uses gelatin instead of the traditional pigskin
to solidify the soup.

1. Combine the water, chicken, pork loin, ham, scallions, ginger,
rice wine, and salt in a large pot. Place the pot over high heat,
and bring to a boil
for 1 minute.
Reduce the heat to
medium-low, and
let the soup simmer
uncovered, stirring
occasionally, for
about 90 minutes
or until only about
one-third of the
original liquid
remains. Strain
out the solids.

2. Put the warm
soup in a nonmetallic container, and sprinkle the gelatin powder
on the surface. Let it stand for 10 minutes or until the gelatin has
absorbed some liquid and no longer appears powdery. Give the
soup a good stir so that the gelatin dissolves, cover the container,
and refrigerate for at least 3 hours.

6 cups water

1/2 pound bone-in chicken thighs

6 cubes (cut 1 inch square) boneless pork
    loin (about 4 ounces)

1/3 cup Chinese ham or country ham,
    cut in 1/2-inch cubes
    (about 4 ounces)

2 tablespoons coarsely chopped scallions

2 tablespoons coarsely chopped
    fresh ginger

1/4 cup Chinese rice wine

1 packet unflavored gelatin powder
    (see note)

NOTE: Fanatics for authenticity can add a
6-inch square of well-scrubbed pigskin
and leave out the gelatin.

Filling for Shanghai-Style Soup Dumplings

Makes filling for 25 dumplings

1 cup boiling water

1/2 cup dried shiitake mushroom caps
cut into 1/4-inch pieces

1/2 pound ground pork

1 tablespoon soy sauce

1 tablespoon finely minced fresh ginger

2 cloves garlic, minced

1 tablespoon sesame oil

1 tablespoon Chinese rice wine

1. Pour the boiling water over the shiitake pieces, and let them stand for 15 minutes. Drain.

2. Combine the drained mushrooms, ground pork, soy sauce, ginger, garlic, sesame oil, and rice wine in a large bowl, and mix well until all the ingredients are evenly distributed. Refrigerate until you're ready for the next step.

Filling, Forming, and Cooking Shanghai-Style Soup Dumplings

1. Spoon 1 teaspoon of the filling and 1/2 teaspoon of soup (I use a demitasse spoon for this) in the center of a wrapper, and close by pinching the edges (see photos). For the most part, tradition holds that you must use 16 pinches, but other traditional-ists insist that 18 are correct. Whatever you do, make sure your dumplings are well-sealed or else the soup will all wind up at the bottom of the cooking pot.

2. Line a steamer tray with napa cabbage leaves, and carefully place the filled dumplings on them. Make sure the dumplings don't touch either each other or the edges of the pot. Steam over medium heat for 15 minutes (remember, this is pork and has to be completely cooked; see "Make the Sacrifice," page 31), and serve immediately.

NOTE: Provide big spoons and chopsticks so that the dumplings can be carefully lifted from the steamer trays. Experienced eaters know that it's impossible to keep *all* the soup in the dumplings. Because of that, the cabbage lining the steamer baskets has a wonderful braised-in-soup flavor, so instead of discarding them, use them as "placemats" for the dumplings. I've been known to steal them off my wife's plate before she knew what happened.

"Chinese Wheat-Flour Dumpling Wrappers," see page 48

Napa cabbage to line the steamer baskets

Steamed Shiitake and Mustard Green Buns

Makes 24 buns

Yeast-raised buns are the dominant form of dumpling in Flushing, but they are amazingly similar: white bread on the outside and ground pork in the middle (see note). This recipe keeps the basic form but changes the filling to one that's completely vegetable.

WRAPPERS

1 teaspoon sugar

1 cup lukewarm water

1 packet active dry yeast

3 cups all-purpose flour

1 tablespoon vegetable oil

Vegetable oil spray

FILLING

1 tablespoon peanut oil

1 tablespoon soy sauce

1 tablespoon Chinese rice wine

2 cups chopped fresh shiitake mushroom caps (about 6 ounces)

3 cups chopped mustard greens (about 1/2 bunch)

1 tablespoon sesame oil

Napa cabbage leaves to line the steamer basket

1. To make the wrappers, mix the sugar with the water in a small bowl, making sure it's completely dissolved. Then add the packet of yeast, and stir gently to dissolve in the sugar water. Set aside for 5 minutes so that the yeast can activate.

2. Put the flour in a large bowl and add the yeast liquid and the vegetable oil. Mix thoroughly and then knead it for 5 to 7 minutes or until it's a dough.

3. Lightly spray a large, clean bowl with vegetable oil spray, and add the dough. Cover the bowl with a damp towel, and leave it someplace where it won't be disturbed for 3 hours. At that point, it should have more than doubled in size.

4. To make the filling, heat the peanut oil in a wok or large skillet over high heat. Add the soy sauce and rice wine. This liquid will cool down the pan a bit, so let it reheat, and then add the mushrooms. Cook and stir for about 2 minutes or until the mushrooms are browned and take on that cooked-mushroom texture. Mix in the mustard greens, and continue stirring—they don't call this "stir frying" for nothing!—until the leaves turn dark green and the stems are fork tender. When the filling mixture is done, remove from the heat, set it aside, and let cool.

5. To finish the wrappers, roll the risen and expanded dough into a cylinder, and then slice it into 10-inch-long plugs. Form each piece into a ball. On a floured work surface, roll out each ball of dough into a thin disk about 5 inches in diameter (use a large cookie cutter or a small bowl as a template). A piece of parchment paper between the dough and the rolling pin will make things a bit easier.

6. Spoon a tablespoon of filling into the center of a dough disk, and form it into a dumpling by pinching the edges of the disk and making little pleats (see photo at right).

7. Line your steamer basket with a single layer of napa cabbage leaves, and steam the dumplings over high heat for 15 minutes or until the filling is completely cooked (see "Make the Sacrifice," page 31). If you're using the stackable bamboo steamer inserts, rotate them every 5 minutes so that each layer gets a chance to be close to the heat. Serve warm.

Cooking Variation
These dumplings can also be baked. While stuffing the dumplings, preheat your oven to 425 degrees. Coat a baking sheet with vegetable oil spray, and place the filled dumplings on the sheet. Bake for 15 minutes or until a deep-brown crust has formed. Allow them to cool for at least 5 minutes before serving.

NOTE: To make the pork variation, use "Steamed Chinese Pork Dumplings (shu mai)" filling instead (see page 56).

63

Wontons Served Three Ways

This must be one of the world's most popular dumpling types. They're served in all sorts of Chinese restaurants—from hole-in-the-wall takeout shops to fancy places with linen tablecloths—and on every continent. In the Asian center of Flushing, Queens, they're served three ways: in soup, deep fried, and boiled with a hot chili sauce. All of those presentations are right here. But first the basics: wrappers and filling.

Chinese-Style Egg-Pasta Wonton Wrappers

Makes 60 wrappers

3 cups all-purpose flour plus flour for the work surface

2 eggs

1. Combine the flour and eggs in a large bowl, and mix thoroughly. If dough hasn't formed from the egg alone, add hot water 1 tablespoon at a time until it does. Knead the dough for about 5 minutes or until it's elastic. Form the dough into a ball, wrap it in plastic, and refrigerate for at least 30 minutes.

2. On a floured work surface, roll out the dough into a large, rectangular sheet. Running the dough through a pasta machine will help, but it won't become as thin as Italian pastas; these have much more egg and/or some oil. Cut the sheets into 3-inch squares, and place them between pieces of parchment paper so that they don't dry out. If you're not going to fill the wrappers immediately, refrigerate the squares.

3. Use in any recipe that calls for wonton wrappers.

Wonton Filling

Makes filling for 60 wontons

1. To make the filling, combine the pork, cabbage, bamboo shoots, garlic, scallions, soy sauce, sesame oil, and pepper together in a large bowl. Mix together very thoroughly so that all the ingredients are evenly distributed. Remember: This is raw meat, so it needs to be kept in the refrigerator if not cooked immediately.

2. Using 1 teaspoon of filling per wonton, put the filling in the center of a square of wrapper dough. Fold the dough in half to form a triangle. Press out any air that's trapped around the dough and seal the edges by pinching and pressing. Then, form a small kink on each short edge of the triangle. Fold the two bottom corners of the triangle together. Seal them to the main body with a drop of water if needed.

FILLING

1 pound ground pork

2 cups finely chopped napa cabbage

1/2 cup minced bamboo shoots
(about 2 ounces)

2 cloves garlic, finely chopped

1 tablespoon minced scallions

2 tablespoons soy sauce

1 tablespoon sesame oil

1/2 teaspoon ground white pepper

WRAPPERS

"Chinese-Style Egg-Pasta Wonton
Wrappers," page 64

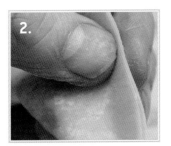

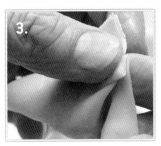
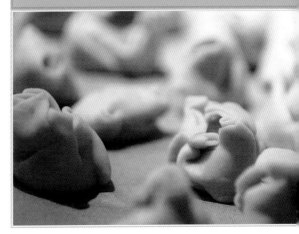

Wonton Soup

Makes 4 servings

Although wontons can be served in all sorts of broths, chicken is most common.

1 quart chicken broth

2 tablespoons soy sauce

1 tablespoon rice wine vinegar

1 tablespoon sesame oil

16 prepared wontons

Deep-Fried Wontons

This is the richest and most luxurious way to serve them.

3 quarts vegetable or peanut oil

16 prepared wontons

Combine the chicken broth, soy sauce, vinegar, and sesame oil in a large pot, and bring to a boil. Add the wontons, return to a boil, and then reduce the heat to a simmer. Continue cooking for 5 minutes, giving the wontons an occasional gentle stir to make sure that they don't stick or come apart. Serve immediately.

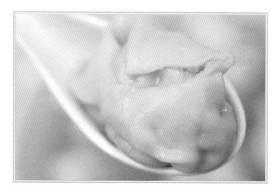

1. Heat the oil in a heavy pot over medium or medium-high heat, and stir occasionally until the oil reaches 375 degrees. Gently lower the wontons into the hot oil, using a slotted spoon or wire basket. Continue cooking for about 5 minutes or until the wontons are golden brown and the meat inside is fully cooked (see "Make the Sacrifice," page 31). Remove from the oil using the same utensil you used to put them in. Drain on paper towels before serving.

2. Serve with "Soy-Vinegar Dipping Sauce," see page 70.

Wontons in Hot Chili Oil

Makes 2 main-dish or 4 appetizer servings

This method from Sichuan is for people who have a love of spicy foods. They can be served as an appetizer or even a main course.

1. Bring the water and the salt to a rolling boil, and add the wontons using a slotted spoon or wire basket. When the water returns to a boil, lower the heat to a simmer, and cook for 5 minutes, stirring occasionally. Remove the wontons from the water using the same utensil you used to put them in, and drain.

2. Combine the chilies in oil, peanut oil, and sesame oil together, and mix well. Set aside for at least 30 minutes to allow the flavors to combine.

3. To serve, pour the oil mixture over the wontons, and sprinkle with the scallions and sesame seeds.

6 quarts water

2 tablespoons salt

20 prepared wontons

1/4 cup ground chilies in oil

1/4 cup peanut oil

1 tablespoon sesame oil

1 tablespoon chopped scallions

1 tablespoon sesame seeds

Everybody's Old Favorite: Wonton Soup

People often ask me what the world's most popular dumpling is, and it didn't take that much thought to come up with an answer: wontons. It may well be that wontons aren't even the most eaten dumpling in China, but wonton soup is found wherever Chinese restaurants have opened—and that's just about everywhere.

Sadly, I couldn't visit some of the more legendary places where wonton soup is said to be served; Greenland and Peru come to mind immediately. Instead, I tried it in a host of small towns across Pennsylvania, Maryland, and Ohio and even in local takeout shops that seemed to specialize in serving non-Asians.

It didn't take much exploring before I proved my theory. Towns that had never seen a pierogi or an empanada often had several Chinese restaurants. They seemed to prepare a standard wonton: much larger than an "authentic" one, with a thicker wrapper, almost no seasoning, and a much stronger meat flavor. Biting into them, you could sense the missing garlic and feel the porkiness. In a half-eaten wonton, the large, complex wrapper folds looked like a maze and the filling, more like a little meatball.

My head was spinning. Was this a sort of baby-food wonton? An easygoing wonton? A garlicless coward's wonton? Or maybe it was a well-fed, contented person's wonton.

As I visited college-town storefronts and farm-village buffets—even a truck-stop snack bar—there was everything I was looking for. The local people were choosing more than just wonton soup, though: steamed and fried dumplings, pickled vegetables, and a host of items that 10 or 15 years ago were only found on big-city Chinatown menus.

It wasn't all authentic. I also started to notice a form of wonton that I'd never seen before: the fried-cheese wonton. This was a typical fried wonton on the outside, with the sauce from macaroni and cheese as filling. Biting through the crisp and nicely greasy wrappers into the unctuous and really rich filling was a junk food blast just one notch below a deep-fried Mars Bar.

All this led to a revelation: Chinese food here has improved—and not just in a few immigrant enclaves. I ate very good pork dumplings in a small Pennsylvania town off I-80; enjoyed Sichuan specialties in Berks County, Pennsylvania; and sadly had to pass up (because I'd already overeaten) even more dumplings in DuBois, Pennsylvania, an almost abandoned but rebounding industrial town. Wherever I went, there were dumplings waiting.

Chinese-Style Spinach Dumplings

Makes 30 dumplings

While dumplings filled with spinach aren't always available, they're always a treat when they turn up. This recipe calls for precooking the ingredients so that they only need a few minutes of steaming or boiling before being eaten.

1. To make the filling, heat the oil in a wok or frying pan over medium heat. Add the ginger, garlic, mushrooms, scallions, soy sauce, and rice wine, stirring for about 5 minutes or until the garlic begins to turn golden. Add the spinach, making sure that the seasonings and greens are well combined and evenly distributed. When the filling mixture is done, remove from the heat, set it aside, and let cool.

2. Fill the dumplings using the "Pinched Half-Moon Method": Form a series of pinches in the edge of the dough about 1/4 inch across. When about half the circle is closed, fold over the other half, and seal the halves together (see instructions on page 25).

3. Line your steamer basket with a single layer of napa cabbage leaves, and steam the dumplings over high heat for about 5 minutes or until the dough in the wrappers is completely cooked. Serve immediately.

Cooking Variation
Spinach dumplings can also be boiled or pan fried. Use the "Half-Moon Fold" (see page 25) in this case.

FILLING

1 tablespoon vegetable oil

1 tablespoon finely chopped fresh ginger

3 cloves garlic, finely chopped

1 cup chopped fresh mushrooms (about 4 ounces)

2 tablespoons chopped scallions

2 tablespoons soy sauce

1 tablespoon Chinese rice wine

2 packages (10 ounces each) frozen, chopped spinach

WRAPPERS

"Chinese Wheat-Flour Dumpling Wrappers," page 48 (Note: Also see the side-bar on page 52) for coloring info)

Napa cabbage leaves for steamer basket

Soy-Vinegar Dipping Sauce

Makes 1/2 cup

1/4 cup soy sauce

3 tablespoons Chinese black vinegar

1 tablespoon sesame oil

2 cloves garlic, finely chopped

1 teaspoon finely chopped fresh ginger

1/2 teaspoon sugar

Optional: hot chili oil

Combine the soy sauce, vinegar, sesame oil, garlic, ginger, sugar, and optional hot oil in a bowl, mix well, and refrigerate for at least 1 hour so that the flavors can combine and develop properly. Serve with dumplings at room temperature.

Side Dish: Sichuan Pickled Cabbage

Makes 8 servings

Korean isn't the only Asian cuisine to serve a side of cold, marinated cabbage with its dumplings. This recipe uses Sichuan peppercorns for their unusual numbing zing.

1. Combine the water with the salt and vinegar in a glass jar or nonmetallic bowl.

2. Toast the peppercorns in a dry skillet over medium heat for 5 minutes. Remove from the heat, set aside, and let cool.

3. Add the cabbage to the vinegar and water mixture. Mix in the red pepper, the toasted peppercorns, and the garlic. Make sure that all the ingredients are well combined and evenly distributed.

4. Cover and refrigerate for 2 days so that the flavors can combine before serving.

1 cup water

1 tablespoon salt

1/4 cup rice wine vinegar

2 teaspoons Sichuan peppercorns

8 cups napa cabbage cut into 1-inch squares (about 1 pound)

1 tablespoon crushed red pepper

6 cloves garlic, crushed

Making Wontons with the Chen Family

Not long after I put the word out that I needed help with my wonton-making skills, I was introduced to Kathy Chen. She's one of those human dynamos who seem to be everywhere these days. With a husband and two small children, and at least two businesses (including managing the modeling career of her son), she thought she could easily find a few hours to teach me more about wontons; in fact, her whole family would come to my kitchen and give me a gang lesson.

Before I could even take the ground pork out of the fridge, the whole Chen family was at my door—mom, dad, grandma, and two adorable children—and they were ready to make dumplings. Soon I was caught up in the action. Every cookie sheet in my house was quickly covered with dumplings, and even the toddler was cranking them out. I took pictures, and took notes, too, and when it was over, I could do nothing but bow at their feet.

They even helped to clean up.

Shrimp and Cucumber Spring Rolls

Shrimp and Cucumber Spring Rolls

Makes 8 spring rolls

Served as appetizers in Vietnamese restaurants, spring rolls almost seem like a dumpling stuffed with salad.

FILLING

1 tablespoon salt for cooking the shrimp plus 1 teaspoon for seasoning

1/2 pound raw medium shrimp, unshelled and deveined

1 tablespoon finely chopped fresh mint leaves

1 tablespoon finely chopped fresh Thai basil leaves

1 tablespoon finely chopped fresh coriander

2 tablespoons lime juice

1/2 teaspoon ground white pepper

1 medium cucumber, cut into matchstick-sized pieces

1 bunch scallion greens, cut into the same length as the cucumber

WRAPPERS

"Round Rice Paper Spring Roll Wrappers," page 80

Bowl of warm water

1. To make the filling, heat a pot of water to boiling, adding the tablespoon of salt. Put the shrimp into the boiling water, and cook for 1 minute. Remove with a strainer, and cool to room temperature. In a bowl combine the cooked shrimp with the remaining 1 teaspoon salt, the mint, basil, coriander, lime juice, and white pepper, and mix well. Refrigerate for at least 30 minutes so that the flavors can combine.

2. Now take a spring roll wrapper, and quickly dip it in the bowl of warm water. The wrapper should soften in about 10 seconds. Place it on a flat work surface, and put 2 tablespoons of the shrimp mixture, a bit of cucumber, and a few pieces of scallion into the center. Roll up the wrapper, and fold the sides like you were gift-wrapping a poster tube. Chill the finished rolls until serving time.

3. Serve the spring rolls cut in half, and put a small bowl of dipping sauce (recipe follows) alongside.

Spring Roll Dipping Sauce

Makes 2/3 cup

Combine the fish sauce, lime juice, chilies, brown sugar, garlic, ginger, and carrot in a container with a lid that can be tightly closed. Mix well, cover, and let stand for at least 1 hour so that the flavors can combine.

4 tablespoons fish sauce

1/4 cup lime juice

2 small fresh green chili peppers, finely chopped

1 tablespoon brown sugar

2 cloves garlic, finely chopped

1 tablespoon finely chopped fresh ginger

2 tablespoons shredded carrot

Thai-Style Herbed Shrimp and Pork Dumplings

Thai-Style Herbed Shrimp and Pork Dumplings
Makes 30 dumplings

In Thailand, nothing is served without some sort of herbal addition, and dumplings like these are no exception.

1. To make the filling, put the shrimp and garlic in a food processor, and pulse several times. Add the shallots, scallions, fish sauce, lime juice, sugar, and basil, and process until everything is well combined. Put the mixture in a bowl, and add the pork, mushrooms, and carrot. Mix until the mushroom and carrot pieces are evenly distributed.

2. Fill the dumplings using the traditional "Half-Moon Fold": Spoon a teaspoon of filling into the center of a round dumpling wrapper, fold the disk in half, and pinch it shut. (See page 25, for more details.)

3. Bring the salted water to a boil in a large pot. Add the filled dumplings to the boiling water using a slotted spoon or wire basket, return to a boil, reduce to a simmer, and cook for about 6 minutes or until the meat is completely done (see "Make the Sacrifice," page 31). Stir the dumplings every now and then to make sure they don't stick but not so often that they burst. Remove the dumplings from the water using the same utensil. Serve with a Thai dipping sauce (recipes follow).

FILLING
1/2 pound raw, peeled shrimp

3 cloves garlic

1/4 cup chopped shallots

2 tablespoons chopped scallions

2 tablespoons Thai fish sauce (nam pla)

1 tablespoon lime juice

1 teaspoon brown or palm sugar

2 tablespoons chopped fresh basil

1/2 pound ground pork

1 cup chopped fresh shiitake mushroom caps (2 ounces)

3 tablespoons grated carrot

WRAPPERS
"Chinese Wheat-Flour Dumpling Wrappers," page 48

6 quarts salted water

Cooking Variation

These dumplings can also be pan fried. Pour some peanut oil into a nonstick frying pan and heat over medium heat. Fry the dumplings in small batches, turning them over frequently. Make sure the meat filling is cooked all the way through; there should be no sign of pink in the middle (again, see "Make the Sacrifice"). The wrappers should be golden brown, and the juices should run clear. Serve with a Thai dipping sauce (recipes follow).

Thai Peanut Dipping Sauce

Makes 2 1/2 cups

This is a bit more elaborate than the simple soy-based recipes, and the long list of ingredients requires that it be for a larger quantity. Luckily, it's just as good on burgers and fries as it is on dumplings.

1/2 cup peanut oil

1/2 cup peanut butter

2 tablespoons Thai red curry paste

1 cup coconut milk

1 tablespoon soy sauce

1 tablespoon Thai fish sauce (nam pla)

2 tablespoons brown sugar

2 tablespoons lime juice

Combine the peanut oil, peanut butter, curry paste, coconut milk, soy sauce, fish sauce, and sugar together in a food processor to ensure that the ingredients form a smooth paste. Add the lime juice a few drops at a time, and taste test to make sure you have the proper blend of acid and spice. Refrigerate for at least 2 hours so that the flavors can combine. Stir again before serving.

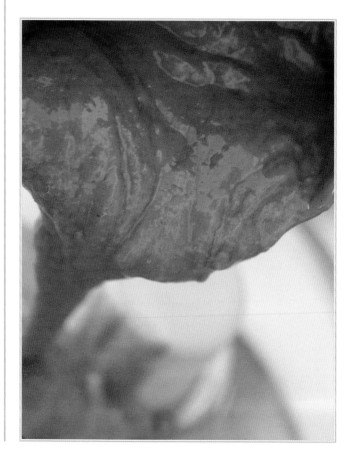

That Other Thai Dipping Sauce (A Jad)

Makes 1 cup

Often when you see Thai peanut sauce on a table, you'll see another item along with it—this one a clear liquid with pieces of cucumber and pepper in it. Both a pickle and a condiment, A Jad somehow manages to be both spicy and refreshing at the same time.

Combine the vinegar and sugar in a nonmetallic bowl, and then add the cucumber, shallots, and peppers. Mix well, making sure that all the ingredients are well coated with liquid. Refrigerate for at least 2 hours before serving so that the flavors can combine.

1/2 cup rice vinegar

1 tablespoon raw sugar

1/2 cup chopped cucumber

1/4 cup chopped shallots or red onion
(2 or 3 shallots or 1/2 small
red onion)

3 whole small fresh chili peppers

Premade Wrappers

You've heard it a million times: Homemade dumpling wrappers are a major key to success. But when push comes to shove, and your shopping cart is drawn toward the packages that you now find in almost every supermarket, you'll reach for premade more often than you'd care to admit. While I would like to urge you to make your own, I buy the commercial ones myself often enough to understand.

Premade wrappers are almost always drier than homemade ones. When using them, keep a small bowl of water handy so that you can wet the edges of the dough before sealing them. And when you're finished, pack up the leftover wrappers quickly; they'll last a couple more days in the refrigerator.

Your Local Asian Grocery: A Shopping List

It used to be that "Asian market" brought to mind a cramped, dingy store in an unfamiliar section of a large city. Today, though, it could just as likely be suburban, big, and modern. Asian markets are often the same size as regular supermarkets, brightly lit, and easy to navigate.

Besides ingredients for the recipes, look for:

CONDIMENTS Black bean sauce, fish sauce, curry paste, oyster sauce, and all sorts of hot sauces are often available for less than half of what they cost in that supermarket across the street. And don't forget soups. Bouillon cube varieties like "Chinese ham," "pork" and "Vietnamese beef" can be a great replacement for their more common equivalents.

COOKWARE Woks, pots, pans, and all sorts of other kitchen tools that you've seen in restaurants but never thought you could find can be had at low prices.

MEAT The quality of chicken, duck, and pork sold in the big Asian stores is often far better than elsewhere in the neighborhood. Portions are smaller and easier to handle, too. Fresh fish can also be good, but the real star is frozen seafood; shrimp, squid, crayfish, and even octopus are always available. Yes, frozen is not as good as properly handled and really fresh, but compare it to what's sold as "fresh" in your community before you pass judgment.

PRODUCE These days everybody seems to know about the greens, but there's more. Look for mushroom varieties like shiitake and maitake as well as fruits like Asian pears, lichees, and durians.

MORE IMPORTANTLY Rice. Long grain, short grain, white, brown, black, red, sweet, sushi . . . .

Coriander Chutney

Indian Triangular Fried Dumplings (Samosas)

Walk through any South Asian neighborhood in this country, and chances are you'll see people eating this triangular-shaped fried dumpling. It can be stuffed with potatoes or other vegetables for vegetarians or ground lamb for meat eaters.

Samosa Wrappers

Makes 24 wrappers

1. Put the 3 cups of flour and the salt in a large bowl, and stir to combine. Add the oil, and then use your fingers to press the oil and flour together, working the mixture into a ball. Add water 1 tablespoon at a time until a dough forms. On a floured work surface, knead the dough for about 5 minutes or until it becomes elastic. Again, form the dough into a ball, spray the ball of dough with oil, cover with plastic wrap, and let it rest for about 30 minutes.

2. To make the dumplings, see "Filling, Forming, and Cooking Samosas," below.

Filling, Forming, and Cooking Samosas

1. Divide the ball of dough into 6 smaller balls—each will become the wrapper for 2 samosas—and roll each ball into a thin disk. Cut the disk in half so that you have 2 half-circle-shaped pieces of dough. Roll a piece into a cone (see photos), and add 2 tablespoons of filling. Fold over the top, and seal the edges.

2. To deep fry the samosas, fill a heavy pot 3 inches deep with corn oil, and heat to 350 degrees. Carefully lower the samosas into the oil using a slotted spoon or wire basket, and cook for about 4 minutes or until the crust is a deep golden brown. Drain on paper towels before serving.

3 cups all-purpose flour plus flour for the work surface

1 teaspoon salt

1/2 cup corn oil

Vegetable oil spray to finish the dough

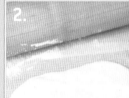

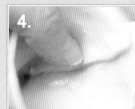

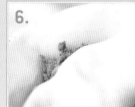

The Samosa Log

Sunday, October 02, 2005. I'm supposed to have complete recipes and photos for samosas, the triangular Indian dumplings most often filled with vegetables or ground lamb. Since I live in a place with a large Indian population, I decide to put up posters around town, asking for help. Several hours later, a sixtyish and very un-Indian looking woman came knocking on my door and said, "You've spelled this wrong. It's 'mimosa' with an M, and you make it by mixing champagne and orange juice."

Monday, October 03, 2005. Nobody else responds to my poster. I spend some time studying samosas at a local Indian restaurant but am eyed with so much suspicion that I can't bring myself to ask anybody anything. I take a few dismal photos of a Styrofoam bowl of samosa chaat while a four-year-old boy watches.

Tuesday, October 04, 2005. Despite leaving messages with people whom I suspect have real influence in the New Jersey samosa community, my phone remains silent. The only things I cook today are hamburgers. My wife pronounces them "awful." I'd better get back on my game here.

Thursday, October 06, 2005. The manager of my condo community phones and tells me that I must remove the posters "right now" or risk a fine. It's just as well. Nobody responded, and, of course, nobody has returned my phone calls, either.

Despite—or because of—all this, I drive down to an old favorite Indian snack shop, order up a batch of samosas, and start dissecting. The flickering fluorescent lights in the shop make photography impossible, and, as always, nobody is willing to

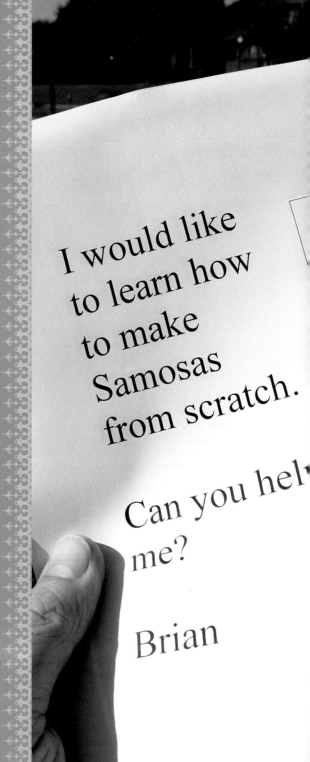

I would like to learn how to make Samosas from scratch.

Can you help me?

Brian

answer a single question. But by the time I've picked apart and eaten the sixth one, I'm an expert and confident I can re-create them at home.

When I'm back out on the sidewalk, I realize that I've consumed over eight million calories (no wonder the women at the counter laughed when I washed it all down with a diet Pepsi), and am so stuffed that I can't figure out how to get back into my car.

Saturday, October 08, 2005. I am unable to even look at a samosa, but I've drafted a complete set of recipes. Only cowardice keeps me from cooking up a batch.

Monday, October 17, 2005. It's over a week later, and while I've eaten and dissected over a dozen more samosas, I've yet to cook anything. But . . . in the early afternoon, a strange and inexplicable force pulls me into an Indian supermarket. I'm convinced that the other shoppers are all thinking, "There's the lunatic who's making samosas from scratch." The few moments I spend dancing to the Bollywood background music does nothing to improve my public image.

By five-thirty that evening, I'd made the dough and filling and tasted my first homemade samosa. It turns out that while the folding method is quite different than what I was used to, it wasn't complex at all (see photos on page 83).

Later, a wave of sadness comes over me as I realize that even on my first try, I have exceeded the quality of almost every local restaurant. Could I ever go into an Indian snack shop again? Of course, if I avoid them, it would free up about six hours a week of my time.

Tuesday, October 18, 2005. During my morning workout, I flip on the TV for some company and find a famous chef making samosas. Stopping and watching for a moment, I realize that either I've got it right or he's got it wrong. This is strangely comforting.

Friday, October 21, 2005. I have now pretty much completed the samosa segment of the book. There are now tested recipes and photos, but word of my quest for an expert has reached some sort of network of Indian food enthusiasts, and I am now receiving many inquiries from them.

Tuesday, October 25, 2005. For the past several days, I've had a flurry of e-mails and phone calls with all sorts of offers. One woman tells me about her mother, who's available only a few hours a month, while another wants to do it but isn't interested in being photographed nude. Finally, there's some headway when I speak with an Indian cooking instructor at a well-known school. She tells me that she is interested in working with me and would be happy to meet in Manhattan this afternoon.

I slog through a chilly fall drizzle to our meeting point: an Upper East Side chain coffee shop. There I sit alone for two solid hours, listening as the servers discuss faith and prophecy among themselves. Meanwhile, what seems like millions of other freelancers are closing deals at every other table. I struggle mightily to avoid falling into an abyss of self-pity as the cooking instructor fails to show up.

Tuesday, November 1, 2005. I get an e-mail from the daughter of the woman who's available only a few hours a month. She's willing to do a photo shoot on Sunday evening and even sends me her address and phone number. I pack my camera bag.

Sunday, November 6, 2005. After over a month of searching, begging, and cajoling, I finally get to visit the home of a woman who's legendary for her samosas and kachoris. Hers was the sort of apartment you'd imagine a culinary master lived in: perfectly clean and filled with the perfume of Indian food.

Yamini was just the sort of person I wasn't: totally efficient and perfectly organized. Within moments of my arrival, and while I was still plugging in my camera's flash unit, she had begun to assemble the ingredients for several classic dumplings from a pantry cart that looked like it was just wheeled in from a cooking-show taping.

Along with a full-time job and school in the evenings, this woman runs a catering business and cooks almost every meal her family eats from scratch. I want to hear more about her story—coming to New York City from Rajasthan—but she is whizzing around the kitchen explaining and demonstrating every aspect of the samosa-maker's art, from the kneading of dough to deep frying.

I leave feeling like a welcomed and well-sated pilgrim and go home to incorporate many of her techniques, from the details of seasoning to the use of corn oil, into the book's recipes. Best of all, though, were the photos—a real chance to take a close look at a master at work.

Spicy Vegetarian Samosas

Makes filling for 12 samosas

Indian dishes combine traditional ingredients with New World imports like potatoes and chilies. But this dish is more than spuds, and with peas, cauliflower, and all those spices, an explosion of taste and texture is present in every bite.

FILLING

1 cup diced potatoes (about 1 large potato); Yukon Golds are favorites here

1/4 cup corn oil

1/8 teaspoon ground asafetida

1 teaspoon whole fennel seeds

1 teaspoon whole cumin seeds

1 teaspoon whole black mustard seeds

1/4 teaspoon whole fenugreek seeds

2 tablespoons finely chopped dried chili peppers (about 2 peppers)

1/2 cup frozen peas, thawed

1/2 cup finely chopped fresh or frozen cauliflower florets

1/2 cup blanched or frozen chopped spinach

1/2 teaspoon ground turmeric

2 teaspoons salt

1 tablespoon white vinegar

WRAPPERS

"Samosa Wrappers," page 83

1. To make the filling, microwave the diced potatoes on high for about 4 minutes or until they are fork tender. Set aside and let cool.

2. Heat the oil in a deep skillet. When it gets very hot, put in the asafetida, and stir it for about 10 seconds. Then add the fennel, cumin, black mustard, fenugreek, and chilies, stirring for 1 more minute. Add the potatoes, peas, cauliflower, spinach, turmeric, salt, and vinegar, and lower the heat to medium. Cook and stir for another 15 minutes or until the cauliflower is tender and the spices have permeated all the vegetables. Drain off any excess liquid, set aside, and let cool.

3. Follow the directions for "Filling, Forming, and Cooking Samosas" on page 83.

4. Serve with Coriander Chutney (see page 98) or as a chaat (see page 91).

Ground Lamb Samosas

Makes filling for 24 samosas

Samosas filled with ground lamb are a popular snack in Pakistan and in meat restaurants in India.

1. To make the filling, heat the oil in a deep skillet. When it's very hot, cook the ginger, pepper, cumin, turmeric, chili, and salt, stirring for about 1 minute. Lower the heat to medium, add the onion, and stir for about 3 minutes or until the onions are both translucent and fully coated with the spice mixture. Add the lamb, and continue cooking for about 15 minutes or until the meat is well browned. Drain, set aside, and let cool.

2. To make the dumplings, see "Filling, Forming, and Cooking Samosas," page 83.

3. Serve with both Coriander Chutney (see page 98) or as a chaat (see page 91).

FILLING

3 tablespoons mustard oil

3 tablespoons finely chopped fresh ginger

1 teaspoon freshly ground black pepper

1 tablespoon ground cumin

1 tablespoon ground turmeric

1 tablespoon chili powder

1 teaspoon salt

1 cup finely chopped onion
    (about 1 medium onion)

1 pound ground lamb

WRAPPERS

"Samosa Wrappers," page 83

A Big Piece of Little India:
Saturday Afternoon, Oak Tree Road

If Oak Tree Road were in Los Angeles or New York, it would be a thriving tourist destination. Its huge concentration of restaurants, groceries, jewelry stores, and music and video shops would be mentioned frequently in newspapers and magazines and draw thousands of visitors. Oak Tree Road isn't in a major city, though; the sorts of places that once would have made great ethnic neighborhoods have become too expensive for recent arrivals from India, Pakistan, and Bangladesh to afford. So this vibrant community sits smack in the middle of Central New Jersey's semi-suburban/semi-industrial sprawl that's the towns of Woodbridge, Iselin, and Edison. Isolated by miles of tract houses, warehouses, townhouses, and just plain suburban houses, many people who live only a few miles away don't even know it exits.

Exist it does, though, and on Saturday afternoons, there's a buzz in the air as crowds fill the streets with talk, music, and food. The place is a fashion statement— you'll see every level of South Asian dress, from teenagers in jeans and sneakers accessorized with wristfuls of bangles to gray-haired grannies in faded pastel saris and generations of women under Islamic cover.

There are lots of things to buy on Oak Tree Road—jewelry, electronics, phone cards in whole stores that seem devoted to them—but the moment you set foot here, you are seduced by the fragrance of cooking. First the spices grab you, then maybe kebabs of chicken, lamb, or shrimp. But when you take a look at what people are eating, the most popular item is that Indian dumpling, the samosa.

Those samosas are available for takeout in groceries and sold in snack shops two different ways: a few on a plate with a sweet, brick-red chutney or in a bowl with a mixture of yogurt, hot and sweet sauces, peas or beans, and spices. This glorious mess is called "samosa chaat" (see page 91). Either way, it's worth the trip.

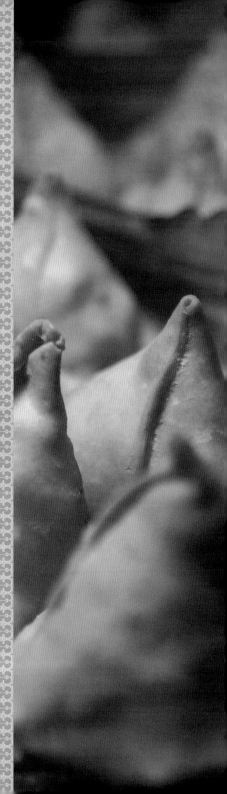

Samosa Chaat

Makes 4 servings

For some of us, samosas are good enough to be eaten straight, but there's another way: served in a bowl with sauces, seasonings, and, in this case, chickpeas. Is this gilding the lily or frosting the cake?

1. Place 2 samosas in eachof 4 soup bowls, and mash them a bit with the back of a spoon. Sprinkle them with the chickpeas.

2. Combine the yogurt, chutney, and chopped mango in a large bowl, and mix until uniform. Pour some of this mixture over the samosas.

3. Sprinkle each serving with the amchur, chili, coriander, and mint. Serve immediately.

8 samosas (see pages 88 and 89)

1 cup cooked chickpeas

1 cup plain yogurt

1/2 cup date, mango, or tamarind chutney

1/4 cup finely chopped green mango or 2 tablespoons mango pickle

1 teaspoon amchur powder

1 teaspoon chili powder

2 tablespoons finely chopped fresh coriander leaves

2 tablespoons finely chopped fresh mint leaves

Potato Parathas

Makes 8 parathas

Do parathas belong in a dumpling book? Well . . . sometimes. Not all are stuffed in the dumpling sense, but here's a recipe for one that is.

WRAPPERS

3 cups all-purpose flour

1 teaspoon salt

1 1/2 cups boiling water

FILLING

1 tablespoon mustard oil

1 tablespoon ground cumin

1 teaspoon dried fenugreek leaves

1/2 teaspoon ground turmeric

1/2 teaspoon garam masala

1/2 teaspoon salt

1 cup finely chopped onion
   (about 1 medium onion)

2 tablespoons finely chopped fresh
   green chili peppers (about
   3 small chili peppers)

2 cups cooked peeled potatoes (about
   3 medium potatoes; see note)

1/4 cup chopped fresh coriander
   leaves

Cooking oil or spray for pan frying
   the filled parathas

NOTE: Local Indian shops sell Idaho potatoes for this purpose. To precook, microwave on high for about 6 minutes or until fork tender. After cooling, they can then be easily peeled and crumbled.

1. To make the wrappers, put the flour and salt in a large bowl, and mix in the boiling water. Use a wooden spoon at first to get the mixture well blended. When the mixture has cooled a bit, knead it for about 7 minutes or until a poke with a finger causes it to bounce back like a soft pillow. Cover the dough in plastic wrap, and refrigerate for about 30 minutes.

2. To make the filling, heat the oil in a wok or skillet over medium heat. Add the cumin, fenugreek, turmeric, garam masala, and salt, stirring for about 1 minute or until the spices begin to turn fragrant. Add the onion and chilies, stirring for about 3 minutes or until the onions turn translucent. Add the potatoes and use a wooden spoon to make sure they're both mashed and well combined with the onion mixture. Stir for about 3 more minutes. Remove the filling mixture  from the heat, set it aside, and let cool. When cool, mix in the coriander leaves.

3. To make the pancakes, section the dough into 8 pieces, and form the pieces into balls about 2 inches in diameter. On a floured work surface, roll out the balls into thin disks about 6 inches across (use a large cookie cutter or a small bowl as a template). Spoon 2 tablespoons of filling into the center of a disk, and then place another disk on top of it. Use the rolling pin to flatten this sandwich into a pancake, and seal the edges with your fingers.

4. Oil a skillet or flat griddle (a pancake griddle is perfect here), and heat it to medium. Fry the parathas, turning frequently, until they are golden brown on both sides.

5. Serve warm with hot and sweet chutneys. (See the recipe for coriander chutney on page 98.)

Indian Round Fried Dumplings (Kachoris)

At Indian snack shops, samosas aren't the only filled dumplings offered. You can often see another right next to it—a disk of obviously stuffed fried dough that looks a bit like a big ravioli. This is a kachori, the samosa's smaller cousin made much the same way.

Kachori Wrappers

Makes 24 wrappers

2 cups all-purpose flour plus flour
    for work surface

1 cup extra-fine cornmeal

1/4 cup corn oil

1 cup hot water

1. Put the flour, cornmeal, and oil in a large bowl, and add the hot water. Blend the mixture well using a wooden spoon. If the dough is dry and cracking, add more water 1 tablespoon at a time until the dough is moist and springy; if the dough is sticky, add more flour 1 tablespoon at a time until it's smooth. When the dough has cooled a bit, knead it for about 7 minutes or until a poke with a finger causes it to bounce back like a soft pillow. Cover it in plastic wrap, and refrigerate for about 30 minutes.

2. To make the wrappers, slice the dough into pieces about 3/4 inch long, and roll each piece into a ball. On a floured work surface, roll out the ball into a thin disk about 4 inches in diameter (use a cookie cutter or small bowl as a template).

Filling, Forming, and Cooking Kachoris

1. Each kachori requires 2 wrappers, a top and a bottom. To fill, spoon 1 tablespoon of filling (see recipes on pages 96 and 97, or use the samosa fillings on pages 88 and 89) into the center of the dough disk. Then take another disk and place it on top. Seal the edges all the way around, and press it down slightly so that you have something between a Chinese bun and a pancake. Kachoris, like samosas, are deep fried.

2. Fill a heavy pot 3 inches deep with corn oil, and heat to 375 degrees. Carefully lower the kachoris into the oil using a slotted spoon or wire basket, and cook for about 4 minutes or until the crust is deep golden brown. Depending on how large your pot is, you might have to turn them over to fry evenly. Drain on paper towels before serving.

3. As with samosas, serve with both sweet and spicy sauces, such as tamarind and coriander chutneys (see page 98), or as a chaat (see page 91).

Corn oil for frying

95

Corn Kachoris

Makes 12 kachoris

This filling, with its bright colors and crunch, exemplifies everything that's good about Indian snacks.

FILLING

2 tablespoon corn oil

2 tablespoons chopped fresh chili peppers (2 chili peppers)

1 teaspoon cumin seeds

1/2 teaspoon ground turmeric

1/2 teaspoon salt

1 1/2 cups corn kernels

1 cup peas

1 tablespoon lime juice

WRAPPERS

"Kachori Wrappers," page 94

1. To make the filling, cook and stir the oil, chilies, cumin, turmeric, and salt in a heavy skillet on high heat for about 30 seconds or until the chilies begin to soften. Add the corn and peas, and continue cooking for about 5 more minutes or until the vegetables are heated through and the flavors combine. Remove the filling mixture from the heat, add the lime juice, and toss to combine. Set aside and let cool.

2. To make the dumplings, see "Filling, Forming, and Cooking Kachoris," page 95.

Dried Fruit Kachoris

Makes 12 kachoris

Like the corn filling on page 96, this is completely vegetarian.

1. To make the filling, combine the ricotta, cardamom, apricots, figs, pistachios, raisins, and sugar in a bowl, and mix until all the ingredients are well distributed.

2. To make the dumplings, see "Filling, Forming, and Cooking Kachoris," page 95.

FILLING

1 cup low-fat ricotta cheese
(*NOTE:* To be perfectly authentic, you'd use the Indian ingredient called "double milk" or "khoya.")

1/2 teaspoon green cardamom seeds

1/2 cup chopped dried apricots

1/2 cup chopped dried figs

1/2 cup chopped pistachios

1/2 cup raisins

1 tablespoon sugar

WRAPPERS

"Kachori Wrappers," page 94

Coriander Chutney

Makes 1 cup

This is the perfect dipping sauce for samosas, kachoris, and parathas. Indeed, some people like it so much that they wind up putting it on steaks and baked potatoes, too.

1 cup coarsely chopped fresh coriander leaves

2 tablespoons shredded unsweetened coconut

2 fresh green chili peppers, stems removed

2 whole garlic cloves

2 tablespoons coarsely chopped fresh ginger

1/4 cup lime juice

1/2 cup corn oil

1/2 teaspoon salt

Combine the coriander, coconut, chilies, garlic, ginger, lime juice, corn oil, and salt in a blender, and process for about 2 minutes until liquefied. Add water 1 tablespoon at a time if needed. Refrigerate for at least 3 hours before serving so that the flavors can combine and develop.

NOTE: Remember that this chutney is fresh and doesn't have the shelf life of the bottled products you buy in stores; it needs to be kept refrigerated.

CENTRAL ASIA
AND THE
MIDDLE EAST

Uzbek Meat Dumplings (Pelmini)

Is There Really a Little Uzbekistan?

In other times—and in other places—the people of Uzbekistan were known as serious gastronomes. Before the ascendancy of "fine-dining" restaurants in Paris, London, Tokyo, and New York, Uzbeks used their location to create what is truly one of the world's first fusion cuisines.

The dumplings here tell the story: Chinese shapes, dough made with milk, and the word "samsa" are each a link to a different culture. This is a crossroads and the first stop on the Silk Road after leaving China.

Almost everything about a typical Uzbek restaurant screams Russia or Eastern Europe, but there are those anomalies. Isn't that carrot salad a bit like kimchi? (See page 44.) Doesn't that bread look Indian—they even make it in a tandoor! And then there's the soup. Everybody's eating the soup, and when they put it in front of you, your head spins—this is Chinese! Or at least this *looks* Chinese . . . until you taste that Chinese-looking soup, and its flavors are completely western. Soy sauce is replaced by salt and pepper, and the broth isn't that different from what American or European home cooks aspire to every time they haul out the stockpot.

Many things have been said about the Uzbek people, but nobody ever called them "masters of marketing." In the neighborhoods of Forest Hills and Rego Park in the New York City borough of Queens, where Uzbek culture is said to flourish, I didn't see a single sign that mentioned the work "Uzbek." Instead, storefront restaurants and food shops—often lit so brightly that they seemed like operating theaters and patronized by people who looked Indian and spoke Russian—merely said "Kosher" or "Kosher Middle Eastern."

I stopped in a plain storefront marked "Kosher Restaurant," ordered a bowl of pelmini soup, a meat samsa, and a plate of carrot salad while a very strange feeling of déjà vu washed over me. Had I been Uzbek in another life? No . . . during my childhood more than 40 years ago, this place was a red-sauce Italian restaurant that my family ate in frequently. The walls were the same color, the paintings were at least in the same style, and the arrangement of tables was unchanged.

Today, the area is a magnet for Asian and Eastern European immigrants, and only a few traces of its past as the almost suburban middle-class residential neighborhood of my boyhood remain. I wandered the streets looking for what's left. At the subway station on Queens Boulevard, I found it—in dumpling form, of course: a shop selling knishes (see page 169), a specialty from the Eastern European Jewish tradition.

Even when there are no other clues, dumplings tell the story.

Uzbek Meat Dumplings (Pelmini)

Makes 80 dumplings or 8 servings

In a good, strong chicken broth—a great use for homemade broth—these tiny dumplings make an amazingly satisfying soup. It's served in a typical meal with salad, bread, and, if the diners are very lucky, some kebabs of marinated meat.

WRAPPERS

3 cups all-purpose flour
    plus flour for work surface

1 egg

1 cup milk

FILLING

1/2 cup finely chopped onion
    (about 1 small onion)

2 cloves garlic, finely chopped

1 pound ground lamb (see note)

1 teaspoon salt

1/2 teaspoon freshly ground
    black pepper

6 quarts salted water

8 cups chicken broth

4 tablespoons chopped fresh
    Italian parsley

4 tablespoons chopped fresh dill

NOTE: Substitute ground beef
if you must.

1. To make the wrappers, mix the flour, egg, and milk in a large bowl. Use a wooden spoon to get the ingredients well blended. If the dough is dry and cracking, add more milk 1 tablespoon at a time until it's moist and springy; if the dough is sticky, add more flour 1 tablespoon at a time until it's smooth. Then knead the dough for about 7 minutes or until a poke with a finger causes it to bounce back like a soft pillow. Cover the dough in plastic wrap, and refrigerate for about 30 minutes.

2. Form the rested dough into a cylinder about 3/4 inch in diameter, and then slice it into sections about 1/8 inch thick. On a floured work surface, roll out each section into a thin disk about 2 inches in diameter. The wrappers are now ready for filling.

3. To make the filling, mix the onion, garlic, lamb, salt, and pepper in a large bowl. Make sure that the ingredients are well combined and evenly distributed.

4. Fill the dumplings using the traditional "Half-Moon Fold" (see page 25).

5. Bring the salted water to a boil in a large pot. Add the dumplings to the boiling water using a slotted spoon or wire basket. Return the water to a boil, reduce to a simmer, and cook for 6 minutes or until the meat is completely cooked (see "Make the Sacrifice," page 31), stirring every now and then to make sure the dumplings don't stick to the pot but not so much that they burst. Meanwhile, heat the chicken broth.

6. To serve, put 1 cup of the broth in a soup bowl and add 10 pelmini. Sprinkle with 1/2 tablespoon each of the chopped parsley and the dill, and serve immediately.

Why Must Pelmini Be So Tiny?

As you struggle to make to make these little folds, you'll almost certainly wonder why pelmini have to be so tiny. Unlike Chinese dumplings with similar ingredients, these contain raw onion, which takes a bit of energy to cook. Because heat penetrates small objects more quickly, downsizing them solves this problem handily.

By the way . . . khinkali—Georgian meat and caraway dumplings (see page 116)—also use raw onion but solve the cooking-time problem by grinding it into a pulp first. Same issue, different solution, and completely different flavor.

Sweet Walnut Fritters (Samsa)

Makes 20 samsa

With an Asian-sounding name, sugar and walnuts in the center, and a distinctly Turkish wrapper, samsa are a real fusion dish—but then again, so is nearly everything from this part of the world. This is cooking from the Silk Road.

WRAPPERS

3 cups all-purpose flour plus flour
  for work surface

1 1/2 cups water

1 teaspoon salt

2 tablespoons unsalted butter
  plus 2 tablespoons for
  rolling out the dough

FILLING

1 1/2 cups chopped walnuts

1/4 cup butter, just warm enough
  to melt

1/4 cup sugar

Peanut oil

Powdered sugar

1. To make the wrappers, combine the 3 cups flour, water, salt, and 2 tablespoons of the butter in a large bowl, and stir slowly until well combined. Form the mixture a ball, and knead it on a floured surface for about 3 minutes or until a dough begins to form. If the dough is dry and cracking, add more water 1 tablespoon at a time until it's moist; if the dough is sticky, add more flour 1 tablespoon at a time until it's smooth. Roll out the dough into a flat rectangle about 24 inches long. Brush the top surface with the remaining butter, fold the dough in quarters, and roll it into a 12- x 24-inch-long sheet. Cover with plastic wrap, and set aside. If you're not going to fill the wrappers immediately, refrigerate the dough until ready.

2. To make the filling, toss the walnuts, butter, and sugar together in a bowl, making sure that all the ingredients are well combined and evenly distributed.

3. To make the samsa, cut the dough into 6-inch squares, and spoon a heaping tablespoon of filling into the center. Bring the four corners together over the center, and pinch together. Continue pinching along the seams until everything is sealed.

4. Heat the peanut oil in a heavy pot over medium or medium-high heat, stirring occasionally until the oil reaches 375 degrees. Gently lower the dumplings into the oil using a slotted spoon or wire basket made for this purpose. Cook the samsa until they are golden brown. Remove them from the oil using the same utensil you used to put them in, and drain on paper towels.

5. Dust with powdered sugar, and serve warm.

Meat and Caraway Dumpling

Georgian Soda Breads (Khachapuri)

These are Georgia's grab-and-go foods. In areas where people from the former Soviet Union live, you'll find them sold by street vendors or at deli counters by the cash register as an impulse purchase. In the Brighton Beach section of Brooklyn, New York, people stroll along the boardwalk eating them or run for the subway with a half-eaten khachapuri in hand.

Georgian cooks make khachapuri three different ways: as a sort of giant but kachorilike (see page 95) disk, as fist-sized half moon, and as a square. We use the square here, but don't be surprised if you see the other shapes in restaurants and bakeries. In these recipes we've left South and East Asia behind almost completely. Now there's yogurt, red beans, and feta on the ingredients list and baking as the cooking method.

The same but different . . . .

Khachapuri Wrappers

Makes 12 wrappers

3 cups all-purpose flour plus flour
for work surface

1 teaspoon baking soda

1/2 teaspoon salt

1/2 cup peanut oil

1 cup plain yogurt

1/2 cup milk

Oil or oil spray for the baking sheet

1. Sift the 3 cups flour, baking soda, and salt together, making sure the ingredients are well combined. Add the oil, yogurt, and milk, and mix well until a dough starts to form. If the dough is dry and cracking, add more water 1 tablespoon at a time until it's moist and springy; if the dough is sticky, add more flour 1 tablespoon at a time until it's smooth. Put the dough on a floured work surface, and knead for about 5 minutes or until a poke with a finger causes it to bounce back like a soft pillow. Cover the dough in plastic wrap, and refrigerate for about 30 minutes. (Remember, it has milk and yogurt in it.)

Filling, Forming, and Cooking Khachapuris

1. Preheat your oven to 400 degrees.

2. Divide the prepared dough into 12 equal pieces. Press a piece into a disk, and roll it out flat on a floured work surface until it's thin enough to cut an 8-inch square out of it. Spoon 2 tablespoons of filling, either "Kidney Bean" (page 114) or "Feta and Herb" (page 115) into the middle of the wrapper. Lift a corner of the dough by the edge, and bring it to the center. Repeat with the other three corners so that you have a square base with flaps covering the dough and filling. Pinch the edges of the flaps to seal the khachapuri, and place on a well-oiled baking sheet. Repeat with the remaining pieces of dough.

3. Bake at 400 degrees for 25 minutes or until the crust is golden.

Vegetable oil or vegetable oil spray

Kidney Bean Khachapuris

Makes 6 khachapuris

FILLING

2 tablespoons peanut oil

1 teaspoon whole coriander seeds

1 cup chopped onion
(about 1 medium onion)

1 can (15 1/2 ounces) red kidney
beans, rinsed and drained

1/2 teaspoon salt

1/4 teaspoon freshly ground
black pepper

WRAPPERS

Khachapuri Wrappers, page 112

1. To make the filling, heat the oil in a skillet over medium heat. Add the coriander and onion, and cook and stir for about 5 minutes or until the onions begin to brown at the edges. Stir in the beans, salt, and pepper, and continue cooking for about 10 minutes or until all the ingredients are well mixed and completely heated through. When the filling mixture is done, remove from the heat, set it aside, and let cool.

2. To make the dumplings, see "Filling, Forming, and Cooking Khachapuris," page 113.

Feta and Herb Khachapuris

Makes 6 khachapuris

1. To make the filling, combine the butter and egg yolk in a large bowl. Mix until they form a paste. Dice the egg whites and add, and then add the farmer cheese, feta cheese, mint, tarragon, salt, and pepper, mixing until all the ingredients are well combined and evenly distributed. Refrigerate until ready to use.

2. To make the dumplings, see "Filling, Forming, and Cooking Khachapuris," page 113.

FILLING

2 tablespoons butter, at room
     temperature

1 hard-cooked egg,
     white and yolk separated

1 cup farmer cheese

1/2 cup crumbled feta cheese

2 tablespoons chopped fresh mint

2 tablespoons chopped fresh tarragon

1/2 teaspoon salt

1/4 teaspoon freshly ground
     black pepper

WRAPPERS

Khachapuri Wrappers, page 112

Meat and Caraway Dumplings

Makes 15 dumplings

No matter how much you read about khinkali, these meat-and-caraway dumplings from Georgia, nothing can prepare you for the first time you see them. They look Chinese—*really* Chinese—they use "Chinese Wheat-Flour Dumpling Wrappers" (see page 48), and employ almost exactly the same folding technique (except for a little tab at the top). But Georgians use caraway seeds, onions, and cayenne, giving us another one of those Silk Road variations.

1. To make the filling, mix the onion, pork, beef, the teaspoon of salt, pepper, and caraway seeds in a large bowl until everything is evenly combined. If you're not making the dumplings right away, store the filling in the refrigerator.

2. Spoon a heaping tablespoon of filling into the center, of each wrapper and fold the dumpling by pinching the edges, exactly as you would a large "Shanghai Soup Dumpling" (see the step-by-step photos on page 61). When you finish, give the top an extra pinch to create a little tab.

3. To cook, put the 2 tablespoons of salt in the water, and bring to a boil. Place the dumplings into the pot using a slotted spoon or wire basket. Return the water to a boil, lower the heat to simmer, and cook, stirring occasionally, for 12 minutes or until the meat filling is completely done (see "Make the Sacrifice," page 31). Gently remove the dumplings with the same utensil you used to put them in, and serve warm with a bit of yogurt on the side.

NOTE: Leftover cooked khinkali can be reheated by frying in butter.

FILLING

1 cup pureed onion (about 2 medium
    onions; see note 1)

1/2 pound ground pork

1/2 pound ground beef

1 teaspoon salt plus 2 tablespoons salt
    for the cooking water

1/2 teaspoon cayenne pepper

1 teaspoon caraway seeds, crushed
    (see note 2)

6 quarts water

NOTE 1: Use a meat grinder, blender, or
food processor for this.

NOTE 2: To crush the caraway seeds,
put them in a plastic bag and smash
them a couple of times with a
meat mallet.

WRAPPERS

"Chinese Wheat-Flour Dumpling
    Wrappers," page 48

To Paterson with Salam

After being baffled a few too many times in the Arabic shops and restaurants of Paterson, New Jersey, I asked my old friend Salam—an American-born child of Lebanese immigrants—to join me on a tour of stores and bakeries and help make sense of things. In the snack bar of one of the largest supermarkets, we ordered a huge plate of variously filled pies, and he began to talk about his childhood, the food in front of us, and Arab flavors in general.

"As a kid, I wanted McDonald's," he confessed, "but I didn't even get to try it till high school." There was an occasional trip to Roy Rogers, but in his house, it was his mom's cooking that ruled. Homemade flatbreads, grape leaves picked from wild vines, and, of course, those little pies.

Picking up a spinach pie from the big platter, Salam announced, "These taste exactly like the ones mom made." I took a bite and found a refreshing acidity; it was the lemon. Indeed, I recalled buying and squeezing them for the recipe (see page 123).

I might have been thinking about flavors, but Salam's memories of childhood—inspired by the plateful of pies—were in full gear. As he munched on them, he spoke more about his mom's cooking and her little-known cuisine. "Mom's pies were much smaller than these," he said as he hefted one. He told us that she filled them with spinach, meat, and potatoes. Meat-and-potato pies were in short supply that day, though. Instead we had (besides spinach) olive and pine nut, and a filling made with soft cheese.

"Mom would take a whole day to make bread and pies," Salam continued. "On those days we just went through the kitchen a lot. Mom called us 'saws' because we'd go back and forth and take little pieces."

I told myself that we were taking home a bag of those big triangular spinach pies so that I could get better photos of them, but Salam began eating them almost before I could set the lights up. Soon my wife, Maria, wandered in with deep concern on her face; would there be any left to bring to work the following day? Or would we have to go back (a 60-mile drive) for more?

Spinach Pie from a local bakery

Middle Eastern–Style Pies

When noon rolls around on Main Street in Paterson, New Jersey, you can see waves of people drifting towards the bakeries. There, in brick ovens that look more suited to a pizzeria, they turn out tray after tray of meat and vegetable filled "pies." But they're not in pie tins and not sold in slices. Instead, they're sheets of dough wrapped around savory or sweet fillings—dumplings by my definition.

Yeast Pie Wrappers

Makes 12 wrappers

1 1/2 cups water (see note)

1 teaspoon sugar

1 packet active dry yeast

4 cups all-purpose flour plus flour
     for kneading

1 teaspoon salt

1/4 cup olive oil plus oil for the
     rising bowl

NOTE: If in doubt about the quality of your water, use bottled or filtered; if your dough isn't rising properly, this is the first issue to examine.

1. Heat the water to about 100 degrees, and mix in the sugar and yeast. Let stand at room temperature for about 10 minutes or until the yeast begins to bubble and froth.

2. Combine the yeast liquid, the 4 cups of flour, the salt, and the 1/4 cup of oil in a large bowl, and mix until a thick dough forms. If the dough is dry and cracking, add more water 1 tablespoon at a time until it's moist and springy; if the dough is sticky, add more flour 1 tablespoon at a time until it's smooth. On a floured work surface, knead the dough for about 7 minutes or until a poke with a finger causes it to bounce back like a soft pillow. Oil a bowl, put in the dough, cover it with a towel, and let it rest for 3 hours or until it has doubled in size. Then divide the dough into 12 smaller pieces, form each piece into a ball, and roll out each ball into a thin disk about 6 inches in diameter (use a large cookie cutter or a small bowl as a template).

3. The pie wrappers are now ready for filling and baking.

Leek Pie

Makes 12 pies

Don't worry about all those leeks and onions. The ingredients will shrink quite a bit during cooking.

1. To make the filling, heat the oil in a large skillet over medium heat. Add the garlic, chili pepper, and sumac, cooking and stirring for about 5 minutes until the garlic turns golden at the edges. Add the leeks and onions and continue cooking, occasionally stirring, for about 30 minutes or until the onions start caramelizing. Mix in the coriander, lemon juice, salt, and pepper, making sure that all the ingredients are well combined. Remove the filling mixture from the heat, set it aside, and let cool.

2. Spoon 2 tablespoons of filling into the middle of each prepared wrapper. Then lift the halves, and pinch them together. Keep pinching the dough shut until you have a large half-moon-shaped dumpling (see page 25).

3. Preheat your oven to 325 degrees.

4. Coat or spray a cookie sheet with olive oil, and lay out the pies on it. Bake for about 45 minutes or until the crust turns golden. The pies can be served right away, but they also keep for several days in the refrigerator.

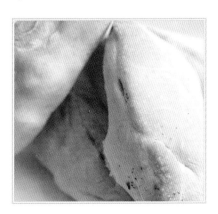

FILLING

2 tablespoons olive oil

6 cloves garlic, crushed and chopped

1 tablespoon finely chopped fresh
    chili pepper

2 tablespoons ground sumac

3 cups chopped leeks
    (about 1 large bunch)

2 cups chopped yellow onions
    (2 large onions)

3 tablespoons finely chopped fresh
    coriander leaves

1/4 cup lemon juice

1 teaspoon salt

1/2 teaspoon freshly ground black pepper

WRAPPERS

"Yeast Pie Wrappers," page 120

Olive oil for baking

Chickpea Pie (Fatayer bi Hummus)

Makes 12 pies

OK . . . how many of you thought that "hummus" was the Arabic word for a creamy, starchy dip that went with pita bread? Well, *I* did. But this little pie isn't filled with creamy stuff. Instead, it's got whole chickpeas.

FILLING

1 1/2 cups dried chickpeas, soaked overnight in 2 quarts of water

1 tablespoon salt

2 quarts water

2 tablespoons chopped fresh Italian parsley

1/2 teaspoon freshly ground black pepper

WRAPPERS

"Yeast Pie Wrappers," page 120

Olive oil for baking

1. To make the filling, put the soaked and drained chickpeas and salt in a pot with the cooking water, and bring to a boil over high heat. Let the chickpeas boil for 1 minute; then lower the heat to a simmer and cook, covered and stirring occasionally, for 2 hours or until the chickpeas are very tender. You don't want them al dente. Drain the chickpeas, and mix in the parsley and pepper.

2. Spoon 2 tablespoons of filling into the middle of the prepared wrappers. Imagine a triangle in the dough circle; bring the three corners of the triangle together, and pinch them tight. Seal the pies by pinching the dough edges together. (See photos.) With any luck, you'll end up with nice little triangles.

3. Preheat your oven to 325 degrees.

4. Coat or spray a cookie sheet with olive oil, and lay out the pies on it. Bake for 45 minutes or until the crust turns golden.

Spinach and Pine Nut Pie

Makes 12 pies

People are always amazed at how universal some foods are. Pork, chicken, and wheat are eaten by a big chunk of the world's population—but if I had to choose one food as the most widespread, it would be spinach. You'll find it everywhere! Always the same leafy green but with some local twist. Here's the Arab take on Popeye's favorite vegetable.

1. To make the filling, heat the oil in a large skillet over medium heat. Add the onion and pine nuts, and cook and stir for about 10 minutes or until the onions turn brown at the edges. Add the spinach, lemon juice, sumac, salt, and pepper and cook for 2 more minutes or until the ingredients have blended together.

2. Spoon 2 tablespoons of filling into the middle of the prepared wrappers. Imagine a triangle in the dough circle; bring the three corners of the triangle together, and pinch them tight. Seal the pies by pinching the dough edges together. (See photos on page 50.) With any luck, you'll end up with nice little triangles.

3. Preheat your oven to 325 degrees.

4. Coat or spray a cookie sheet with olive oil, and lay the pies on it. Bake for 45 minutes or until the crust turns golden

FILLING

1 tablespoon olive oil

1 cup chopped onion (about 1 medium onion)

1/2 cup pine nuts

4 cups chopped cooked spinach (about 3 pounds fresh spinach; see note)

1/4 cup lemon juice

1 tablespoon ground sumac

1 teaspoon salt

1/2 teaspoon freshly ground black pepper

NOTE: Frozen chopped spinach works well here; you'll need about two-thirds of a 20-ounce bag.

WRAPPERS

"Yeast Pie Wrappers," page 120

Olive oil for baking

Your Local Arab Grocery: Deals to Watch For

On rare occasions, I'll go shopping in search of an unusual or sublime ingredient; other times, I'll need to stock up the pantry; and, finally, there are days when I'm just looking for a bargain. That's when I find myself heading down to the strip of Middle Eastern and Turkish groceries in Paterson, New Jersey.

The most obvious good deal is olive oil. Stores there sell good oil for 20 or 30 percent less than supermarkets. The same rules for quality apply here: Look for "extra virgin" as the best. Lower grades, often just marked "olive oil" or "pomace oil," are useful for recipes that call for frying, but they don't deliver the same flavor.

Oil isn't the only bargain, though. The olives themselves are often half the price of ones of similar quality in Italian or gourmet stores. And then there's what Turkish chefs call "white" cheese and we call "feta." Here you'll find feta in a wide variety from subtle (or at least subtle by feta standards) to extra pungent. There's also another bonus: Because whole olives and feta are staple foods in this part of the world, you'll be assured of freshness and authenticity.

And don't overlook the bakery sections. These days, everybody knows pita bread, but how many of you know that it's just a small part of a much larger Arab baking tradition? Look for everything from tiny pastries the size of a half dollar to flatbreads 18 inches across. Needless to say, you'll find familiar packages of pita at prices so low, you'll get mad the next time you're in the supermarket.

Pistachios, hazelnuts, and dates are also basic staples in this part of the world, and they're bargains, too. In bulk bins, cans, or plastic bags, these items and their prices will make you happy you came.

Are there exotic items here? Yes, and lots of them—sumac powder, all sorts of cheeses, pickles, sauces, and jams—but it's those bargains that bring me back. After all, I eat bread and olive oil every day.

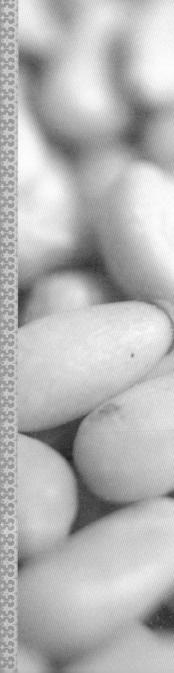

(Turkish Ground-Meat Dumplings (Manti)

Turkish Ground-Meat Dumplings (Manti)

Makes 50 manti

Manti don't really look like other dumplings. They're folded like tiny samsas, but then they're boiled, not baked. The name is clearly linked to Korean "mandu" and the Chinese word "mantou," both dumpling names. Of course, the yogurt sauce with sumac makes the dish Middle Eastern beyond question.

1. For the yogurt sauce, mix the yogurt, garlic, and salt together in a bowl, and refrigerate for at least 4 hours to let the flavors combine. Give the sauce a stir every half hour or so.

2. For the wrappers, combine the flour, egg, and salt with the water, and mix well. If the dough is dry and cracking, add more water 1 tablespoon at a time until it's moist and springy; if the dough is sticky, add more flour 1 tablespoon at a time until it's smooth. On a floured work surface, knead the dough for about 4 minutes or until the dough becomes a bit elastic. Then cover the dough in plastic wrap, and refrigerate for about 30 minutes.

3. Press the dough flat, and run it through a pasta machine (see "Pasta Machine 101," page 21) until you get very thin sheets. Cover the sheets with a damp towel until you're ready to use them, as they dry out very quickly.

4. For the filling, mix the onion, beef, parsley, salt, and black pepper in a medium bowl until all the ingredients are well combined and evenly distributed. If you're not going to fill the wrappers immediately, refrigerate the mixture until ready.

5. Make the final topping by heating the oil, Aleppo pepper, and sumac in a small skillet over medium heat. Cook and stir until the oil begins to sizzle and all the spices are well coated. Remove from heat, set aside, and let cool.

6. Form the manti by cutting the dough sheets into 1-inch squares. Spoon 1/4 teaspoon of filling into the middle of a square, and bring the corners together. (See the photos on page 50. Also check out " Sweet Walnut Fritters (Samsas)" on page 108 for a giant version of the same fold.)

7. Salt the water and bring it to a boil in a large pot. Using a slotted spoon or wire basket, add the manti. When the water returns to a boil, lower it to a simmer, and partially cover the pot. Cook for 6 minutes or until the meat is completely done (see "Make the Sacrifice," page 31). Remove the dumplings with the same utensil you used to put them in. Drain.

8. To assemble the manti, place the just-cooked dumplings on a plate, cover with the yogurt-garlic sauce, and drizzle the pepper-sumac topping over it all. Serve immediately.

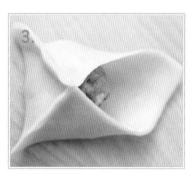
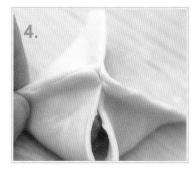

SAUCE

2 cups yogurt

1 tablespoon finely chopped garlic

1/2 teaspoon salt

WRAPPERS

2 cups all-purpose flour

1 egg

1/2 teaspoon salt

3/4 cup water

FILLING

1/2 cup grated onion
(about 1 small onion)

1/2 pound ground beef

1/4 cup finely chopped fresh Italian
parsley

1 teaspoon salt

1/2 teaspoon freshly ground black pepper

2 tablespoons olive oil

1 teaspoon Aleppo pepper or Hungarian
paprika

1 tablespoon ground sumac

6 quarts water

2 tablespoons salt for boiling

Side Dish: Turkish Coffee

Makes 2 demitasse cups

One of the thrills of heading over to the Turkish and Arabic neighborhoods of Paterson, New Jersey, and Brooklyn, New York, was the coffee. As sweet as candy and black as night, it was the perfect drink to sip after an intensely flavored pastry.

When you stroll around places like these, you'll see *ibriks*— the tiny, long-handled Turkish coffee pots—for sale everywhere. You'll need the coffee, too. Besides being the darkest of dark roasts, it's ground into a fine powder especially suited for this style of preparation.

> 1/2 cup cold water
>
> 2 tablespoons very finely ground coffee
>
> 2 teaspoons sugar (see note)
>
> 1 green cardamom pod, crushed
>
> *NOTE:* You can use more or less sugar if you wish, but this amount gives a degree of sweetness that's about the same as a typical neighborhood Turkish restaurant.

1. Put the water, coffee, sugar, and the cardamom pod in your ibrik, give it a couple of stirs, and place it over low heat. Do not stir again! Soon, the coffee will float to the surface and form a crust, and after 3 or 4 minutes, a foam will break through. When the foam fills the pot to the top, take it off the heat, spoon the foam into cups, and pour the coffee into the cups without disturbing the foam. (I get my best results pouring down the side of the cup in the same way many people fill beer glasses.)

2. Serve immediately. Otherwise, you'll wind up with murky glop on the bottom and brown sugar water on top.

RUSSIA
AND
EASTERN EUROPE

Beggar's Purses

Little Russian Pies (Piroshki)

On the streets of Brighton Beach in Brooklyn, you'll find these sold by the same street vendors who offer khachapuri (see page 111) and other popular foods from the old Soviet Union. Here, we've got the classic yeast-raised wrapper and both meat and mushroom piroshki.

Piroshki Wrappers

Makes 20 wrappers

Meant to warm you up in cold weather, this is as much a bread as a wrapper—a rich and chewy enclosure for those deeply flavored fillings.

1 1/2 cups water (see note)

1/2 teaspoon sugar

1 packet active dry yeast

3 cups all-purpose flour plus
        flour for work surface

2 tablespoons butter, warmed to room
        temperature

1/2 teaspoon salt

2 tablespoons milk

1 egg

Vegetable oil or vegetable oil spray
        for the rising bowl

NOTE: I find that I get much better results using bottled water because the chlorine in my tap water kills the yeast before it can rise.

1. Warm the water to about 100 degrees, and mix in the sugar and yeast. Let stand at room temperature for about 10 minutes or until the yeast begins to bubble and froth.

2. Combine the yeast liquid, the 3 cups of flour, butter, salt, milk, and egg in a large bowl, and mix until a thick dough forms. On a floured work surface, knead the dough for about 5 minutes or until a poke with a finger causes it to bounce back like a soft pillow. Put the dough in a well-oiled bowl, cover it with a towel, and let it rest at room temperature for 3 hours or until it has doubled in size.

3. Roll out the raised dough into a 1/8-inch-thick sheet. Then form 3-inch-diameter disks (use a large cookie cutter or a small bowl as a template). The wrappers are now ready to be filled and baked.

Filling, Folding, and Cooking Piroshki

1. Preheat your oven to 375 degrees.

2. Fill the dumplings using the traditional "Half-Moon Fold" (see page 25). Put a tablespoon of filling in the center of a round dumpling wrapper, fold the disk in half, and pinch it shut. Place on a well-oiled cookie sheet, brush the tops with the beaten egg, and bake at 40 minutes or until golden brown. Serve warm, or store in the refrigerator.

Vegetable oil or vegetable oil spray

1 lightly beaten egg for egg wash

Meat Piroshki

Makes 20 pies

These little pies can be street food bought from a vendor, or served in a snack shop with a pot of tea or as an appetizer in a larger meal.

FILLING

1 tablespoon butter

2 cups chopped onion
(about 2 medium onions)

1 pound ground beef

1 teaspoon salt

1/2 teaspoon freshly ground black pepper

1 hard-cooked egg, chopped

WRAPPERS

"Piroshki Wrappers," page 132

1. To make the filling, melt the butter in a skillet over medium-low heat. Add the onions, and cook and stir for about 30 minutes or until they caramelize and turn a deep golden color—you're looking for something about the same as a well-done French fry here. (Don't turn up the heat to save time; you'll just burn the butter.) Add the ground meat, salt, and pepper, and continue cooking for about another 30 minutes or until the meat is cooked through.

2. When the filling mixture is done, remove from the heat, add the chopped egg, mix well, and set aside and let cool.

3. To make the dumplings, see "Filling, Folding, and Cooking Piroshki," page 133.

Mushroom Piroshki

Makes 20 pies

In this part of the world, mushrooms are both a treasure and a staple food. Fancy dried wild ones make this a luxury dish, and plain old button ones make it regular.

1. To make the filling, melt the butter in a skillet over medium-low heat. Add the scallions, cooking and stirring for about 1 minute or until their color brightens. Add the mushrooms, salt, pepper, and dill, and continue cooking and occasionally stirring for about 30 minutes or until the mushrooms turn golden and have reduced to about one-third their original size.

2. When the filling mixture is done, remove from the heat, add the chopped egg, mix well, and set aside and let cool.

3. To make the dumplings, see "Filling, Folding, and Cooking Piroshki," page 133.

FILLING

1 tablespoon butter

1 cup chopped scallions (about 1 bunch)

6 cups chopped fresh mushrooms (about 2 pounds; see note)

1 teaspoon salt

1/2 teaspoon freshly ground black pepper

3 tablespoons chopped fresh dill

1 hard-cooked egg, chopped

NOTE: Regular button mushroom caps will work fine here, but if you can find something a bit fancier, it will really help. Shiitake, oyster, and porcini mushrooms will all give the recipe some added zing.

WRAPPERS

"Piroshki Wrappers," page 132

Beggar's Purses

Makes 15 purses

Almost everybody who's ever read a food magazine has heard of these, but who's actually *eaten* them? Filled with luxury items and generally offered only in places where the displays of expensive ingredients are part of the dining experience, beggar's purses are dumplings that speak of wealth and privilege. Traditionally, the luxury item for most people was wild mushrooms. Yes, beggar's purses can be found with caviar, lobster, truffles, or foie gras, but we'll pass on them for the moment.

1. To make the filling, melt the butter in a skillet over medium-low heat. Add the bacon and garlic, cooking and stirring for about 15 minutes or until the meat begins to turn golden. Add the mushrooms, salt, and pepper, and don't be surprised when the pool of oil formed by the bacon and butter disappears. Continue cooking for about 40 minutes or until the mushrooms are browned and have reduced to about one-third their original size. When the filling mixture is done, remove from the heat, set it aside, and let cool.

2. Preheat your oven to 325 degrees.

3. To form the purses, cut the sheets of rolled-out dough into 4-inch diameter disks (use a large cookie cutter or small bowl as a template), and spoon a tablespoon of filling into the center. Gather the edges together as if you were making a soup dumpling (see page 61) or khinkali (see page 116), but don't seal the edges. Instead, use a scallion green as a sort of string, and tie them shut. Brush the purses lightly with the melted butter don't forget to include the bottoms so that they don't stick to the cookie sheet. Bake for 45 minutes or until the wrappers turn golden.

4. Serve warm with sour cream.

FILLING

1 tablespoon butter plus 2 tablespoons melted butter to finish the purses before baking

1/4 cup chopped bacon

2 cloves garlic, finely chopped

2 cups chopped fresh wild or exotic mushrooms (see note)

1/2 teaspoon salt

1/4 teaspoon freshly ground black pepper

NOTE: Look for porcini, oyster, bluefoot, or other mushrooms in the market.

WRAPPERS

"Sour Cream Pierogi Wrappers," page 152; you only need one-third of the recipe—see note 1)

15 scallion greens (see note 2)

1 cup sour cream as a garnish

NOTE 1: Regular pierogi dough isn't the traditional wrapper of choice here, but it's far easier than the route most restaurants choose: making cornmeal crepes or finding phyllo dough flexible enough to form into purses.

NOTE 2: To use the scallion greens as ties, you'll have to crush them flat so that they don't break when they're bent. Do this by pulling between your thumb and forefinger. If you're the dexterous sort, they can be peeled into smaller strips, but I just did the flattening— anything more, and I messed them up a bit too much.

Side Dish: Korean Salad

Makes 6 servings

In Russian, this is called "Korean Salad," but it doesn't resemble anything you'd find in a Korean kitchen. These marinated carrots—with caraway seeds and dill— are as Russian as a salad can get.

2 tablespoons cider vinegar

1 teaspoon salt

1/2 teaspoon freshly ground black pepper

2 teaspoons caraway seeds

1 teaspoon crushed red pepper

4 cloves garlic, thinly sliced

1 teaspoon ground coriander

3 tablespoons peanut oil

4 cups shredded carrot (about 6 large carrots)

2 tablespoons finely chopped fresh dill

Mix the vinegar, salt, pepper, caraway seeds, crushed red pepper, garlic, coriander, and oil together in a small bowl, and stir well to make sure all the ingredients are evenly combined. Pour this dressing over the carrots and dill, in a large bowl toss, and refrigerate for at least 4 hours so that the flavors can combine. Serve chilled.

Little Ear Dumplings in Borscht (Vushka)

Filled Pastas from Poland and Ukraine: Pierogi and Vareniki

The words "pierogi" and "vareniki" may sound completely different, but they're really the same thing: pasta filled with vegetables, meat, fish, or fruit. They're food staples in Poland (where the word "pierogi" comes from) and Ukraine (home to the word "vareniki," also commonly spelled "varenyky," "varenyki," or "vareniky").

In both Eastern Europe and North America, these dumplings are regularly encountered. They're available premade in supermarkets, at both ethnic and local restaurants, and are a fixture and church and service-club events. In addition, many areas have specialty pierogi shops (see "Masters of the Pierogi," page 156).

So why are some recipes here called "pierogi" and others "vareniki"? The names were chosen based on the first reference found. If sources were from Ukraine, they became vareniki, and if from Poland, pierogi.

Potato Vareniki Wrappers

Makes 50 wrappers

In Eastern Europe recipes are tightly intertwined. This dough appears as a wrapper for both vareniki and pierogi.

1 cup peeled, cooked potato
    (about 1 large potato)

1/4 cup peanut oil

2 cups all-purpose flour plus flour
    for work surface

1 teaspoon salt

1 cup water

1. Run the potato through a food mill or ricer. Combine it with the oil, egg, 2 cups flour, salt, and water in a large bowl, and mix until a dough forms. If the dough is dry and cracking, add more water 1 tablespoon at a time until it's moist; if the dough is sticky, add more flour 1 tablespoon at a time until it's smooth. On a floured work surface, knead the dough for 3 or 4 minutes or until it's elastic. Cover the dough with plastic wrap, and refrigerate for at least 30 minutes. If need be, it can stay refrigerated for several hours.

2. Divide the dough into quarters, and roll them out into flat sheets. Use a pasta machine (see "Pasta Machine 101," page 21), and crank the sheets through until you create a moderately thin dough—number 4 on my machine—and then lay them out on a floured work surface. Cut the dough into 3-inch-diameter disks (use a cookie cutter or small bowl as a template). You can run the leftover dough though the machine once more to minimize waste as long as it doesn't get too dry. (Watch for cracking here— it's the telltale sign.) The wrappers are now ready to be filled and cooked. You'll find that they'll need 2 minutes more than the other wrappers to cook completely.

Ground-Fish Vareniki

Makes 20 vareniki

Traditionally made with freshwater fish, these dumplings can use carp, tilapia, or even salmon.

FILLING

1/2 cup finely chopped onion
    (about 1/2 large onion)

3 cups finely chopped carp or tilapia fillets
    (about 1 pound)

2 tablespoons finely chopped fresh dill

1 teaspoon salt

1/2 teaspoon freshly ground black pepper

WRAPPERS

Either "Sour Cream Pierogi Wrappers,"
    page 152, "Egg- and Dairy-Free
    Pierogi Wrappers," page 153,
    or "Potato Vareniki Wrappers,"
    page 141

1. To make the filling, combine the onion, fish, dill, salt, and pepper in a bowl, and mix well. Since this is raw fish, you have to be careful! Refrigerate the finished mixture, make the dumplings quickly, and don't let the uncooked stuffed vareniki sit out too long.

2. To make the dumplings, see "Filling, Folding, and Cooking Pierogi and Vareniki," page 154.

Farmer Cheese Vareniki

Makes 20 vareniki

Here we use farmer cheese—that drier cousin of cottage cheese—as a filling.

1. To make the filling combine the farmer cheese with the salt, pepper, dill, and egg, and mix well. You'll need something like a pastry cutter or a potato masher and a bit of elbow grease to do it right. The mixture is ready when all the ingredients are evenly distributed. If you're not going to fill the wrappers immediately, refrigerate the mixture until ready.

2. To make the dumplings, see "Filling, Folding, and Cooking Pierogi and Vareniki," page 154.

FILLING

2 cups (two 7 1/2-ounce packages) farmer cheese

1/2 teaspoon salt

1/4 teaspoon freshly ground black pepper

1 tablespoon finely chopped fresh dill

1 egg

WRAPPERS

Either "Sour Cream Pierogi Wrappers," page 152, "Egg- and Dairy-Free Pierogi Wrappers," page 153, or "Potato Vareniki Wrappers," page 141

Cherry Vareniki

Makes 20 vareniki

Most of the dumplings that we've made so far have used meat as a filling. But in this part of the world, people often use fruit. Cherries are an old favorite. Traditionally, they would've used canned, but today they'll just as often use frozen.

FILLING

3 cups pitted fresh, canned, or frozen cherries

2 tablespoons sugar

3 whole cloves

1 tablespoon lemon juice

1 cup water

WRAPPERS

Either "Sour Cream Pierogi Wrappers," page 152, "Egg- and Dairy-Free Pierogi Wrappers," page 153, or "Potato Vareniki Wrappers," page 141

1. To make the filling combine the cherries, sugar, cloves, lemon juice, and water in a saucepan over medium-low heat, and let the mixture simmer uncovered for 30 minutes, stirring occasionally. At this point the fruit should be very soft and thoroughly cooked. Drain in a colander, and then press out any remaining liquid. The results should be the consistency of a good fruit preserve. When the filling mixture is done, remove from the heat, set it aside, and let cool.

2. To make the dumplings, see "Filling, Folding, and Cooking Pierogi and Vareniki," page 154.

Plum Vareniki

Makes 20 vareniki

Plums? Aren't they the same as prunes? Or are prunes a word for dried plums? The answer is "yes" to the last question: dried plums and prunes are the same. Now that we've settled this, let's fill some dumplings with them.

1. To make the filling bring the water to a boil in a saucepan large enough to hold all the ingredients. Add the plums, sugar, lemon juice, cinnamon, and cloves, give it a couple of stirs, return the water to a boil, and then reduce the heat to a simmer. Cook, stirring frequently, for about 10 minutes or until the fruit is very tender. When the filling mixture is done, remove from the heat, extract the cinnamon stick, drain, set it aside, and let cool.

2. To make the dumplings, see "Filling, Folding, and Cooking Pierogi and Vareniki," page 154

FILLING

3 cups water

2 cups chopped, pitted dried plums

1 tablespoon sugar

1 teaspoon lemon juice

1 cinnamon stick

2 whole cloves, pinched

WRAPPERS

Either "Sour Cream Pierogi Wrappers," page 152, "Egg- and Dairy-Free Pierogi Wrappers," page 153, or "Potato Vareniki Wrappers," page 141

The Perfect Cheap Date

For lots of people, "Ukrainian" sounds pretty exotic when it comes to food: maybe something really strange or maybe famine—no food at all. But if you came of age in the early days of Manhattan's East Village resurgence in the seventies, Ukrainian was where you went on cheap dates. If you knew the area, you know what I'm talking about: an afternoon or evening of gallery going followed by visits to the Kiev, the Veselka, and even the obviously named Ukrainian Restaurant, where dumplings were always on the menu.

It was in those places that I would sit over late-afternoon pierogi platters and attempt to convince women that I actually knew something about art and culture. In retrospect, I could have more easily gotten them to believe that I was from Pluto, but somehow, I wanted them to at least think I was smart—and this is what I thought "smart" meant.

On a recent gray January afternoon, I strolled down Second Avenue and was surprised at how much of the Ukrainian presence survived. OK, the Kiev was now a bar, and there were more fancy chain boutiques than you'd find in a good-sized suburban mall, but sure enough . . . there was the Ukrainian Restaurant, down a brightly lit and freshly painted hall at 140 Second Avenue. There was even a sign offering a hot-borscht lunch special and a long list of dumplings marked "Varaniki (Pierogi)."

Up the street was the very cool Veselka Coffee Shop—the site of many of the worst days of my single life. Despite remodeling that made the place look more than respectable, it was still filled with guys who seemed to be working overtime to impress their very bohemian/intellectual-looking girlfriends.

The Veselka counterman snapped me out of my reverie, and I snapped him right back by asking if the "Christmas borscht" contained Ushki. He nodded, smiled, and brought me a bowl: bright-red soup filled with something like tiny wontons. I finished my meal with a platter of unbelievably soothing pierogi. Mild to the point that it was hard to tell their flavor, they remained so comforting that I didn't want to sprinkle salt and pepper on them.

Little Ear Dumplings in Borscht (Vushka)

Makes 50 vushka

These dumplings don't look like human ears. Instead, their name comes from their resemblance to a certain feature of a cat's anatomy. You'll see the similarity, when you make up a batch.

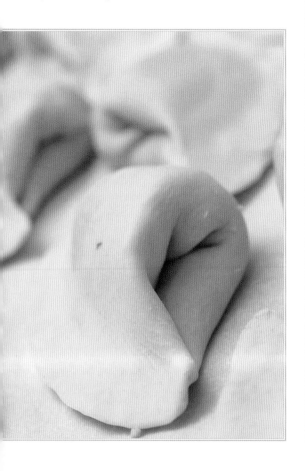

1. For the wrappers, combine the flour, egg, milk, and oil in a large bowl, and mix until a dough forms. If the dough is dry and cracking, add more water 1 tablespoon at a time until it's moist and springy; if the dough is too sticky, add more flour 1 table-spoon at a time until it's smooth. On a floured work surface, knead the dough for 3 or 4 minutes or until it's elastic. Cover the dough with plastic wrap, and refrigerate for at least 30 minutes. If need be, it can stay refrigerated for several hours.

2. Divide the dough into quarters, and roll them out into flat sheets a bit narrower than your pasta machine. Use the pasta machine (see "Pasta Machine 101," page 21), and crank the sheets through until you create a moderately thin dough—number 4 on mine—and then lay them out on a floured work surface. Cut the dough into 3-inch-diameter disks as if you were making pierogi (use a cookie cutter or a small bowl as a template). The wrappers are now ready to be filled and cooked. If you're not going to fill the wrappers immediately, cover them so that they don't dry out.

3. For the filling, heat the oil in a skillet over medium heat. Add the onion, and cook and stir for about 15 minutes or until the edges of the onion turn golden. Add the mushrooms, salt, dill, pepper, and lemon juice, and reduce the heat to medium-low. Continue cooking and occasionally stirring for about 40 minutes or until the mushrooms are browned and have reduced to about one-third their original size. By this time, the mixture will have really shrunk; this is good and concentrates the flavors. When the filling mixture is done, remove from the heat, set it aside, and let cool.

4. Spoon 1/2 teaspoon of filling into the middle of a wrapper, and fold it in half. Seal it around the edges as if it were a pierogi. Then fold it in half again, and pinch the corners where they meet. It will look a bit like an old-style nurse's cap or . . . well . . . a cat's ear.

5. Bring the salted water to a boil in a large pot. Add the filled dumplings to the boiling water using a slotted spoon or wire basket. Return the water to a boil, reduce to a simmer, and cook for about 6 minutes or until the wrappers are completely done and no dough flavor remains when you taste one. Stir every now and then to make sure the dumplings don't stick to the pot but not so much that they burst.

6. To serve, put the hot vushka in individual bowls of borscht, and serve with a dollop of sour cream.

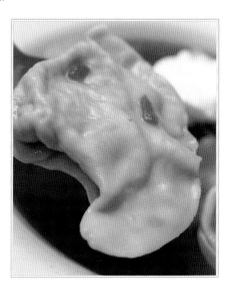

WRAPPERS

3 cups all-purpose flour plus flour for the work surface

1 egg

1 cup milk

1 tablespoon peanut oil

FILLING

2 tablespoons peanut oil

2 cups finely chopped onion (about 2 medium onions)

4 cups finely chopped fresh mushroom caps (see note)

1/2 teaspoon salt

2 tablespoons chopped fresh dill

1/4 teaspoon freshly ground black pepper

1 tablespoon lemon juice

6 quarts salted water

NOTE: Use those supermarket button mushrooms if you must, but shiitake and/or oyster mushrooms will give a much richer flavor.

SERVE WITH

1 cup borscht per person (see "Beef and Beet Broth," page 150)

1 tablespoon sour cream per person

Beef and Beet Broth (Borscht)

It's that red stuff that you find in glass jars on supermarket shelves during certain holidays—the same jars that fruit juice came in decades ago. Bright red, and sometimes with strange little objects floating around—you have to wonder: Is it a soup? A drink? Or something in a class of its own?

It's all of the above. Eastern Europeans have it cold in the summer, hot in the winter, and always with sour cream. Vushka, those little Ukrainian dumplings that look like cat's ears, are served with borscht as a matter of course, but as a side dish, borscht goes with almost everything savory in this section of the book.

True borscht fanatics drink it straight from the jar like some sort of bright-red health tonic, but for the rest of us, a warm bowl with a bit of chopped fresh dill and a dollop of sour cream makes a better choice. Add a handful of vushka (see page 148), or put a big plate of pierogi on the side, and you've got an archetypical Polish or Ukrainian meal.

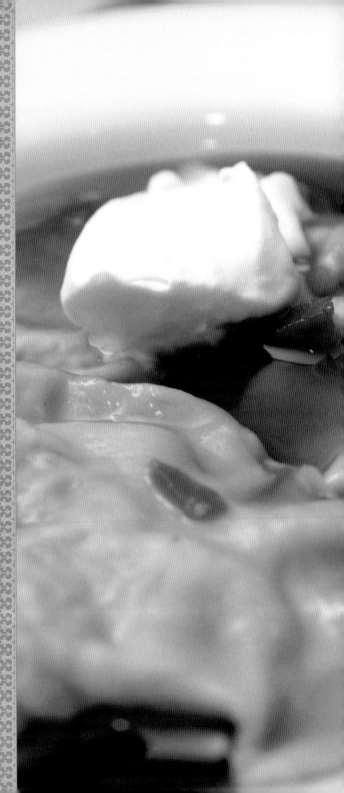

Pierogies frying

Sour Cream Pierogi Wrappers

Makes 50 wrappers

In Eastern European cooking, you'll find fresh dairy everywhere. Here we use sour cream—an ingredient with a unique combination of richness and acidity— to make dumpling wrappers.

3 cups all-purpose flou plus flour for the work surface

1/2 teaspoon salt

1/4 cup sour cream

1 egg

1 cup water

1. Combine the flour, salt, sour cream, egg, and water in a large bowl, and mix until a dough begins to form. If the dough is dry and cracking, add more water 1 tablespoon at a time until it's moist and springy; if the dough is sticky, add more flour 1 tablespoon at a time until it's smooth. On a floured work surface, knead the dough for 3 or 4 minutes or until it's elastic. Cover the dough with plastic wrap, and refrigerate for at least 30 minutes. If need be, it can stay refrigerated for several hours.

2. Divide the dough into quarters, and roll them out into flat sheets. Use a pasta machine (see "Pasta Machine 101," page 21), and crank the sheets through until you create a moderately thin dough—number 4 on my machine—and then lay them out on a floured work surface. Cut the dough into 3-inch-diameter disks (use a cookie cutter or a small bowl as a template). You can run any leftover dough though the machine once more to minimize waste as long as it doesn't get too dry. (Watch for cracking here— it's the telltale sign.) The wrappers are now ready to be filled and cooked.

Egg- and Dairy-Free Pierogi Wrappers

Makes 50 wrappers

If you're one of those people who looks at the eggs and sour cream in the other wrapper recipes with horror, try this one. It's not exactly the same, but you'll still be able to make great dumplings. It comes out much better than dough made from substitute or low-fat products, too.

1. Combine the flour, salt, oil, and water in a large bowl, and mix until a dough begins to form. If the dough is dry and cracking, add more water 1 tablespoon at a time until it's moist; if the dough is sticky, add more flour 1 tablespoon at a time until it's smooth. On a floured work surface, knead the dough for 3 or 4 minutes or until it's elastic. Cover the dough with plastic wrap, and refrigerate for at least 30 minutes. If need be, it can stay refrigerated for several hours.

2. Divide the dough into quarters, and roll them out into flat sheets. Use a pasta machine (see "Pasta Machine 101," page 21), and crank the sheets through until you've created a moderately thin dough—number 4 on my machine—and then lay them out on a floured work surface. Cut the dough into 4-inch-diameter disks (use a cookie cutter or small bowl as a template). You can run any leftover dough though the machine once more to minimize waste as long as it doesn't get too dry. (Watch for cracking here—it's the telltale sign.) The wrappers are now ready to be filled and cooked.

3 cups all-purpose flour plus flour for the work surface

1/2 teaspoon salt

1/4 cup olive oil

1 cup water

Filling, Folding, and Cooking Pierogi and Vareniki

6 quarts salted water

1. To fill the dumplings using the traditional "Half-Moon Fold" (see page 25), spoon 1 teaspoon of filling into the center of a round dumpling skin, fold the disk in half, and pinch it shut.

2. Bring the salted water to a boil in a large pot. Add the filled dumplings to the boiling water using a slotted spoon or wire basket. Return the water to a boil, reduce to a simmer, and cook for 6 to 8 minutes or until the wrapper dough is completely done and there is no doughy flavor left, stirring occasionally to make sure that the dumplings don't stick to the pot but not so much that they burst. Remove them from the water using the same utensil, and transfer them straight to serving plates.

3. Serve warm with sour cream or caramelized onions (see page 161).

Sauerkraut Pierogi

Makes 30 pierogi

Usually, we think of sauerkraut as something that goes on something else—say, the perfect topping for a hot dog or a Reuben sandwich. But with this dish, that sauerkraut is the thing itself.

This is one of those rare times when you'll have an excuse to seek out great sauerkraut. Seize the day! If you're used to the stuff in cans or those plastic bags that seem like stuffed water balloons, it will be a revelation. Look for homemade or store-made sauerkraut in Eastern European shops or imported products in glass jars. You'll finally understand how millions of people can have it as a staple food and really enjoy it. Note that this is one of the few European recipes I've written that rightly doesn't contain salt or pepper. The bacon and sauerkraut season heavily enough as it is.

1. To make the filling, fry the bacon in a skillet over medium heat. When it starts to turn golden, add the onion and keep cooking, occasionally stirring, for about 15 minutes or until the onions are translucent and completely cooked through. Mix in the sauerkraut, and cook for about another 15 minutes or until much of the liquid has evaporated and the flavors have combined. When the filling mixture is done, remove from the heat, set it aside, and let cool.

2. To make the dumplings, see "Filling, Folding, and Cooking Pierogi and Vareniki," page 154.

FILLING

1/4 cup chopped bacon

1 cup chopped onion (about 1 medium onion)

3 cups drained and chopped sauerkraut

WRAPPERS

Either "Sour Cream Pierogi Wrappers," page 152, "Egg- and Dairy-Free Pierogi Wrappers," page 153, or "Potato Vareniki Wrappers," page 141

Masters of the Pierogi

Tucked in among the wooden row houses, strip malls, and industrial buildings of Rahway, New Jersey, is a tiny storefront called the Pierogi Palace. I made my first visit there a couple of days before Christmas and found the roughly 10- by 15-foot shop packed with women making dumplings.

When I asked if I could buy something, I was told, "We have nothing available after November first. People reserve their holiday pierogi way in advance." Indeed, they seemed frantic to the point of incoherence; when explaining the Christmas rush, they told me that "Poles are Catholic, and on Christmas Eve they eat fish—and pierogi are fish." I didn't dare ask for an elaboration of that point. Instead, I watched a woman cut small squares of dough by hand before I quietly left. And it wasn't until after I got back in my car that I realized that every other pierogi I'd ever seen was made with round disks of dough, not little squares.

I didn't return until the week of Valentine's Day. Things at the Palace had calmed down quite a bit, and people were walking in off the street and buying packages of pierogi without much fanfare. It was then that I sat down in the shop and spent some quality time.

Jessica Avent is the Palace's owner, chef, boss, and master craftsperson. With her sister, Jill, mother, Vivian, and friend Debbie helping out, she does everything possible by hand—relying on her senses of sight, touch, taste, and smell, plus everybody's willingness to put in a hard day's work.

Before I was settled in, I couldn't help but notice some big differences in the Palace's pierogi. They're triangular like giant kreplach (see page 164), made from those squares of dough I spotted on my first visit. And not only are they much bigger than most of the other pierogi sold in the neighborhood, they have even more filling. Jessica had strong reasons for this: "If you make them round, you waste lots of dough . . . and if you reroll the dough, it becomes rubbery."

For Jessica, dough is a big topic. "The dough is what makes a pierogi a pierogi; you can't have heavy dough, or you'll have lead sinkers." She continued, "Some people don't have the right texture; they can't work the dough." She's never even tried sour cream or milk, two things that other pierogi chefs swear by. "Eggs, water, flour, salt. Just patience—you'll know when you've got it."

Fillings count, too; potato is by far the biggest seller, but the Pierogi Palace prides itself on special orders: potato and pot cheese, beef brisket, mushroom, mushroom-sauerkraut, and fruit fillings like blueberry, apricot, and plum. The most memorable request was for a special filling made with dried

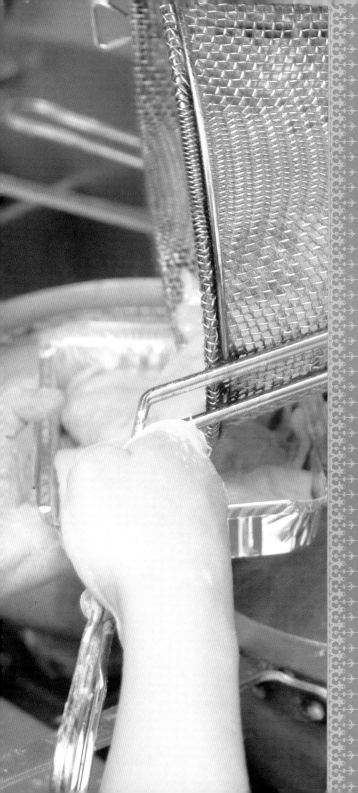

mushrooms imported from Poland. The cost was astronomical (over $100 a pound), and the flavor was absolutely authentic.

But nobody complains about the regular flavors like sauerkraut, potato, or even jalapeño and cheese. Taste tests proved them all to be far more than edible and mild enough for small children. In fact, they were far milder than pierogi in Polish-speaking groceries and delis around town, and when I mentioned this to Jessica, she went on a sort of mildness tirade. "They put salt and pepper on everything—*everything!*—in those places. There's even salt and pepper on mashed potatoes. . . ."

So . . . there's that dough and those fillings, but how are they assembled, cooked, and sold?

The action proceeds rapidly. The dough is rolled out with regular—but huge—rolling pins and filled. Then, without any further delay, they're boiled in water laced with yellow food coloring (to give them the deep color Jessica prizes), sealed into foil pans with clear plastic lids, and cooled down.

Since Jessica is clearly a pierogi fanatic and neither Polish nor Polish American, I thought I'd get her opinion on the biggest pierogi debate of them all: fried versus boiled. "When you fry them, you get the taste of frying but not the taste of pierogi," she explained. "The taste of frying in butter is very good— but we like the taste of our pierogi better."

Cabbage and Mushroom Pierogi

Makes 20 pierogi

Here, two of the most common Polish ingredients are combined in pierogi form. (For an interesting contrast, try the "Chinese Cabbage and Mushroom Dumplings" on page 55 for comparison; really similar ingredients, really different results.)

FILLING

1 tablespoon butter

3 cups shredded cabbage
    (about 1 small head)

2 cups chopped fresh mushrooms
    (about 8 ounces; see note)

1 teaspoon salt

1/2 teaspoon freshly ground
    black pepper

NOTE: Button mushrooms will work fine here, but you can do far better. Try shiitake, oyster, or even portobellas.

WRAPPERS

Either "Sour Cream Pierogi Wrappers," page 152, "Egg- and Dairy-Free Pierogi Wrappers," page 153, or "Potato Vareniki Wrappers," page 141

1. To make the filling, melt the butter in a large skillet over medium heat. Add the cabbage, mushrooms, salt, and pepper, and cook and stir for about 40 minutes or until the edges of the cabbage strips are golden brown. Don't try any shortcuts here! Evaporation and time are what makes this filling work. If you use it before the cabbage has properly browned, it will just be soggy, and if you crank up the heat, it's too easy to burn. When the filling mixture is done, remove from the heat, set it aside, and let cool.

2. To make the dumplings, see "Filling, Folding, and Pierogi and Vareniki," page 154.

Potato Pierogi

Makes 50 pierogi

Even though potatoes are a New World ingredient, they've been grown in Eastern Europe long enough to seem like a traditional staple. These dumplings are just one more way to eat this most basic of foods.

1. To make the filling, heat the oil in a skillet over medium-high heat. Add the onion, and cook and stir for about 10 minutes or until the edges of the onion turn a deep golden brown. Add the scallions, salt, and pepper, and continue cooking for about 1 more minute or until the greens begin to wilt. Add the potatoes, and mix until all the ingredients are well distributed. Break up bigger pieces of potato with a wooden spoon to make things easier to mix. When the filling mixture is done, remove from the heat, set it aside, and let cool.

2. To make the dumplings, see "Filling, Folding, and Cooking Pierogi and Vareniki," page 154.

FILLING

1 tablespoon peanut oil

1 cup chopped onion
    (about 1 medium onion)

1/4 cup chopped scallion greens

1 teaspoon salt

1/2 teaspoon freshly ground black pepper

3 cups peeled, cooked, mashed potatoes
    (about 5 medium potatoes;
    see note)

NOTE: I've had good luck with Yukon Golds.

WRAPPERS

Either "Sour Cream Pierogi Wrappers," page 152, "Egg- and Dairy-Free Pierogi Wrappers," page 153, or "Potato Vareniki Wrappers," page 141

Mushroom Pierogi

Makes 20 pierogi

Mushrooms play an important role in Polish cooking, and this isn't the only Eastern European recipe in this book that uses them as an ingredient. But here they take center stage.

FILLING

1 cup dried boletus mushrooms (see note)

2 cups boiling water

1 tablespoon unsalted butter

2 cloves garlic, finely chopped

1 cup chopped onion (about 1 medium onion)

5 cups chopped fresh button mushrooms (about 1 1/2 pounds)

1/2 teaspoon salt

1/4 teaspoon freshly ground black pepper

1/4 cup finely chopped fresh Italian parsley

NOTE: Look for these mushrooms under their Italian name "porcini" if they don't turn up in an Eastern European store.

WRAPPERS

Either "Sour Cream Pierogi Wrappers," page 152, "Egg- and Dairy-Free Pierogi Wrappers," page 152, or "Potato Vareniki Wrappers," page 141

1. To make the filling, put the dried mushrooms in a heatproof bowl, and pour the boiling water over them. Let them soak for about 20 minutes. Drain, finely chop, and set aside.

2. Melt the butter in a skillet over medium heat. Add the garlic and onion, and cook and stir for about 10 minutes or until the edges of the onions turn golden. Mix in the dried and fresh mushrooms, salt, and pepper, and continue cooking for about 30 minutes or until the mushrooms start to turn golden on the outside. Toss in the parsley, remove the filling mixture from the heat, set it aside, and let cool.

3. To make the dumplings, see "Filling, Folding, and Cooking Pierogi and Vareniki," page 154.

Side Dish: Caramelized Onions

Makes 2 cups

For me, this is a recipe based on magic. With nothing but butter, onions, salt, and pepper, you create something that's almost completely unlike the ingredients you begin with. What is it that makes this work? Time. So have some faith, don't stray too far from the stove, and watch as some onions become wonderful.

Melt the butter in a large skillet over medium-low heat. Mix in the onions, salt, and pepper, and cook, occasionally stirring, until the onions are very soft and the color of caramel candies. Be aware that this takes time. If you've never caramelized onions before, you'll see that it happens in distinct stages:

After the first 30 minutes or so, the onions will just become soggy and collapse into a heap about half the size they were when they entered the pan. If you taste them, you'll get an unmistakable raw onion flavor.

By the end of the first hour, the onions will have shrunk even more and have a tinge of gold. When 90 minutes have passed, they'll have a distinct tan color and a sweet but still oniony flavor and could conceivably be served as is.

After 2 hours, that tan color will deepen, and the edges will start to turn dark brown. The strips of onion will look like dark, soggy noodles. There will be no trace at all of what most people would call "onion" flavor. Instead, it's been replaced by a warm, sugary taste.

At 3 hours, you'll have real caramelized onions. Deep caramel in color (well, what did you expect?) and with complex sweetness. They are the perfect topping for pierogi.

1 tablespoon butter

8 cups thinly sliced onions (about 3 large onions)

1/2 teaspoon salt

1/4 teaspoon freshly ground black pepper

So what happened when I tried speeding things up? First I burned the butter. Then I tried oil, and the onions got darker and crisp and never lost that onion taste. In the end, only the long, slow method worked.

Fried Pierogi

Before I paid a visit to Cleveland's West Side Market, the idea of frying a pierogi never crossed my mind. True, I'd done most of my pierogi eating in New York and New Jersey restaurants that cater to Polish immigrants (my favorite had Polish Olympic memorabilia on the walls, but that's another story), and I never once saw the option of "fried."

It turns out, though, that in the American Heartland, pierogi are fried . . . meant to be fried . . . HAVE to be fried. Deep-fried hot dogs may be a specialty where I live in central New Jersey, but we take our pierogi boiled.

So what's the author of a dumpling book to do? I pulled out my frying pan, put it on the fire with a tablespoon of butter, and threw in some pierogi. The results were gratifying; anybody who likes fried Chinese dumplings would get a similar shot of flavor from these—only with distinctly European seasonings.

Jessica Avent, owner of the Pierogi Palace in Rahway, New Jersey (see page 156), told me that frying them makes them taste more like fried food and less like pierogi, and she was right. But the taste of fried, especially fried in butter, was quite good.

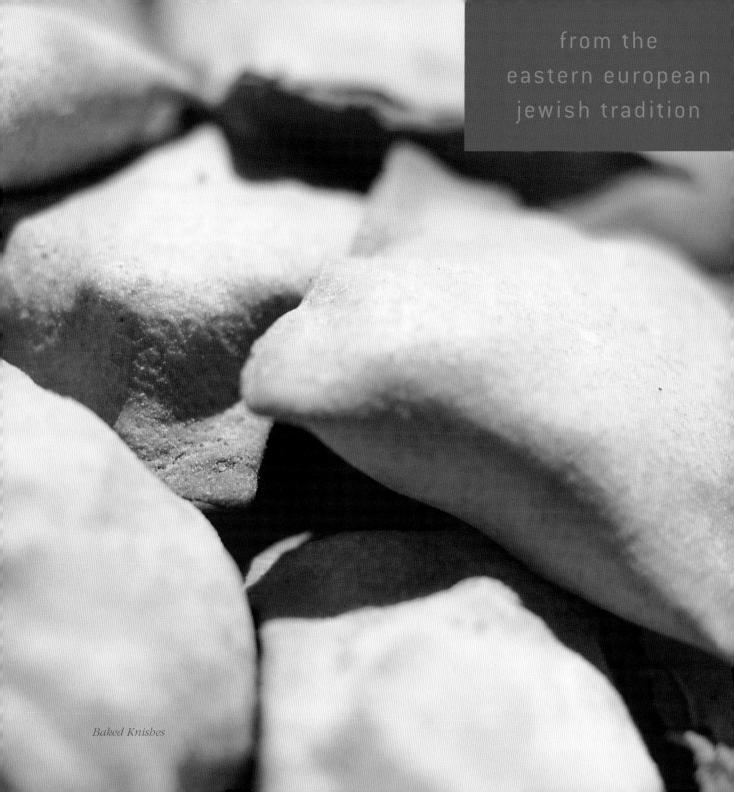

from the
eastern european
jewish tradition

Baked Knishes

Kreplach

A happy dumpling that's associated with holidays especially the Jewish festival of Purim, kreplach are an easy shape to form and great for those who aren't ready for more complex folds.

Two things that always seem to be associated with kreplach and don't appear in my recipes are schmaltz and gribenes. Schmaltz—an ingredient that itself has morphed from rendered goose fat to rendered chicken fat—often seems to be called for. I have noticed that some high-end markets will have small jars of rendered goose fat and that glatt kosher butchers will have schmaltz made from chicken fat. Use these instead of the olive oil I call for when you can, but don't feel obligated. Gribenes (also spelled "gribbens," "grivens," and several other ways) are small pieces of poultry skin that are fried until crisp and seem to make their way into many older recipes, too. If you have some gribenes, just sprinkle them in the filling mixtures right at the end. But like I said, you don't need them; your kreplach will turn out just fine either way.

Kreplach Wrappers

Makes 48 wrappers

Kreplach, like most European dumplings, use a rich, egg-based dough for the wrapper.

2 cups all-purpose flour, plus flour for
      the work surface

2 eggs

1/2 teaspoon salt

1 cup water

1. Combine the flour, eggs, salt, and water in a large bowl, and mix until a dough begins to form. If the dough is dry and cracking, add more water 1 tablespoon at a time until it's moist and springy; if it's sticky, add more flour 1 tablespoon at a time until it's smooth. On a floured work surface, knead the dough for 4 or 5 minutes or until it's elastic. Cover the dough with plastic wrap, and refrigerate for at least 30 minutes. If need be, it can stay refrigerated for several hours.

2. Divide the dough into quarters, and roll them out into flat sheets about the size of a pancake. Use a pasta machine (see "Pasta Machine 101," page 21), and crank them through until you create a moderately thin dough—number 4 on my machine— and then lay them out on a floured work surface. Cut the dough into 2-inch squares. If they have to be set aside, cover with a damp towel to keep them from drying out. The wrappers are now ready to be filled and cooked.

Filling, Folding, and Cooking Kreplach

Like other Eastern European dumplings, kreplach can also be pan fried or even deep fried, but the presentation in soup remains the classic.

1. Spoon 1/2 teaspoon of filling into the center of a dough square, and fold it in half along its diagonal so that you wind up with a triangle. Seal the edges so that no water can leak in and no air pockets remain inside.

2. Bring the salted water to a boil in a large pot. Add the filled dumplings to the boiling water using a slotted spoon or wire basket. Return the water to a boil, reduce the heat to a simmer, and cook for about 6 minutes or until the meat is completely done (see "Make the Sacrifice," page 31). Stir every now and then to make sure that the dumplings don't stick to the pot but not so much that they burst. Remove them from the water using the same utensil, and put them straight into serving bowls.

3. While the kreplach are cooking, warm up the chicken broth and have it ready.

4. To serve, put 1 cup of warm chicken broth and 6 to 8 cooked kreplach in each bowl, and sprinkle with the chopped parsley. Leftover kreplach can be reheated in butter, oil, or even that chicken fat, using a skillet over medium heat.

6 quarts salted water

6 cups chicken broth

1/4 cup finely chopped fresh
    Italian parsley

NOTE: Substitute "Egg- and Dairy-Free Pierogi Wrappers" (page 153) if need be.

Loaves, Fishes, and Even Sauerkraut: Your Local Eastern European Grocery

If you're just going to be making the recipes in this book, there's really no need to visit an Eastern European grocery—but that would be your loss. These stores offer the essentials of hearty cuisine: preserved vegetables and fruits, whole-grain breads, cold cuts, and a wide variety of smoked and pickled fish.

Start in the aisle with those big jars, and look for sauerkraut. You can buy something that seems similar in the supermarket, but one taste and you'll be a convert. I'm also a big fan of the pickled mushrooms and beets. Either of these can be eaten as a simple appetizer or give a plain green salad a nice kick. Great pickled cucumbers of the sort that most of us associate with Jewish delis are often here, too.

For dark, whole-grain breads, an Eastern European grocery is just the right place. Seeded or unseeded rye, pumpernickel, seven-grain, and something brown and mysterious called "health bread" all turn up, and even those that are similar to supermarket varieties—that seeded rye, for example—will be fresher.

Good stores in this genre have something I call "the bucket"—a plastic pail of salted herring fillets. These are inexpensive and can serve as the base of many a great dish. Just don't make the mistake I did: eating them straight from their salty brine without further preparation. If you want something to serve right away, look for the refrigerated jars or plastic packs of herring in wine or cream sauce.

"Kielbasa" or "kielbasy" (Polish for "sausage") are words on plastic-wrapped packages in supermarket meat departments, but when you're at a Polish cold-cut counter, they take on a whole new meaning. From sticks of spicy dried meat smaller than your pinky to salamis the size of baseball bats, the range of cured meats is dazzling. Use them as ingredients for an omelet, a sandwich, or chopped into tiny pieces to fortify a pierogi filling.

One area that always surprises people is the selection of juices. There are the usual orange, apple, and grapefruit, but there are also choices like cherry, carrot, and plum. I suspect this is a modern extension of the need to preserve for the long winter season.

And don't forget to finish things off with dessert; poppy-seed cake is the classic, but there are almost always plenty of what appear to be high-quality pastries with French roots. A tea infused with blackcurrant, peppermint, or lemon is a nice way to end a meal, too.

Chicken Liver Kreplach

Makes 48 kreplach (about 6 servings)

It's hard to believe now, but chicken, goose, and duck livers were once staples of Eastern European Jewish cooking. Goose and duck livers are now expensive luxuries, but chicken livers from organic poultry farms will do a great job here.

1. To make the filling, heat the oil in a skillet over medium heat. Add the garlic and onion, and cook and stir for about 5 minutes or until the garlic and onions turn translucent. Add the chicken livers, and continue cooking until they're browned all the way through. Mix in the egg, salt, and pepper, and give everything a few extra stirs to make sure all the ingredients are well combined. When the filling mixture is done, remove from the heat, set it aside, and let cool. If you're not going to fill the wrappers immediately, refrigerate the mixture until ready.

2. To make the dumplings, see "Filling, Folding, and Cooking Kreplach," page 165.

FILLING

1 tablespoon olive oil

2 cloves garlic, finely chopped

1/2 cup finely chopped onion
    (about 1 small onion)

1/2 pound chicken livers, finely chopped

1 hard-cookd egg, finely chopped

1/2 teaspoon salt

1/4 teaspoon freshly ground black pepper

WRAPPERS

"Kreplach Wrappers," page 164

Beef Kreplach

Makes 48 kreplach (about 6 servings)

Recipes for beef kreplach seem to be in two groups: those that start with raw meat, and those that use leftover cooked meat. I'll use raw here because I just don't know what leftovers you have stashed away.

FILLING

1/2 pound ground chuck

1/2 cup dry bread crumbs

1/2 cup finely chopped or shredded onion (about 1 medium onion; see note)

1/4 cup chopped or shredded carrot (about 1 medium carrot; see note)

1/2 teaspoon salt

1/4 teaspoon freshly ground black pepper

NOTE: Use the shredder disc of a food processor to do this.

WRAPPERS

"Kreplach Wrappers," page 164

1. To make the filling, combine the chuck, bread crumbs, onion, carrot, salt, and pepper in a large bowl, and mix thoroughly, making sure that all the ingredients are well distributed. Don't be afraid to use your hands for this! If you're not going to fill the wrapper immediately, refrigerate the mixture until ready.

2. To make the dumplings, see "Filling, Folding, and Cooking Kreplach," page 165.

Knishes

One of the biggest problems with including knishes in this book was deciding what chapter to put them in. Are they part of the Eastern European Jewish tradition like kreplach? Or are they New York originals like those giant wheels of pizza? Either way, there's filling and dough. . . .

The next issue in unraveling the mysteries of the knish is size. The ones offered in shops in Brooklyn and Queens today are huge—almost certainly the victims of some sort of strange immigrant food inflation that afflicted many cooks who came to this country a century ago. There is no way that we can believe that back in the "old country," a pastrami sandwich contained three pounds of meat, a bagel was five inches across, or a pound of cooked kasha filled only two knishes.

What begins to emerge is a sort of cycle; at one time, knishes were nothing more than baked pierogi. They then grew to become portable, filling meals for immigrant Jewish factory workers, and as their descendants assimilated, the local versions vanished, only to be replaced by what the next batch of newcomers brought: khachapuri (page 111), pierogi (page 154), and piroshki (page 132)— the very same foods that gave birth to the New York knish in the first place.

Knish Wrappers

Makes 30 wrappers

These wrappers are quite similar to the ones used for kreplach (page 164) but with the addition of a bit of whole-wheat flour and baking powder.

2 cups all-purpose flour plus flour for
        the work surface

1 cup whole-wheat flour

1 egg

1/2 teaspoon salt

1 cup water

1/4 cup peanut oil

1/2 teaspoon baking powder

1. Combine the flours, egg, salt, water, peanut oil, and baking powder in a large bowl and mix until dough begins to form. If the dough is dry and cracking, add water 1 tablespoon at a time until it's smooth; if the dough is sticky, add flour 1 tablespoon at a time until it's smooth. On a floured work surface, knead the dough for about 4 or 5 minutes or until it's elastic. Cover the dough with plastic wrap, and refrigerate for at least 30 minutes. If need be, it can stay refrigerated for several hours.

2. Divide the dough into four equal parts, press them flat with your hands, and then use a pasta machine (see "Pasta Machine 101" in "Basics") to crank the sheets through until they become moderately thin—number 4 on my machine—and then lay them out on a floured work surface. Cut the sheets into 3- by 6-inch rectangles. (Most home pasta machines make a sheet 6 inches wide.) If they have to be set aside, cover with a damp towel to keep them from drying out. The wrappers are now ready to be filled and cooked.

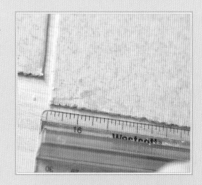

Filling, Folding, and Cooking Knishes

As round as baseballs, as big as grapefruits, square like some sort of construction material, triangles as small as a matchbox or who-knows-what—knishes seem to be all sorts of shapes and sizes. They come in so many forms that the notion of "authentic" is almost a mockery. New York delis sell them round and baked, but New York pushcarts sell them square and fried. Since no two sources can agree on the correct format, *A World of Dumplings* will choose its own: square, about 3 inches across, and baked. Why? The square shape is easier to form and wastes less dough, the 3 inch size is a manageable snack but not so big that it becomes a joke to eat, and while frying leaves its own delicious flavor, baking brings out the best in these simple, mild ingredients.

Vegetable oil or vegetable oil spray

1. Preheat your oven to 425 degrees.

2. Oil a cookie sheet.

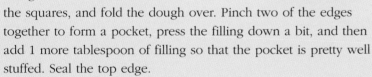

3. Take a rectangle of premade dough, and imagine it divided into 2 squares. Put 1 tablespoon of filling into the center of one of the squares, and fold the dough over. Pinch two of the edges together to form a pocket, press the filling down a bit, and then add 1 more tablespoon of filling so that the pocket is pretty well stuffed. Seal the top edge.

4. Place the formed knishes on the well-oiled cookie sheet, and bake for 30 minutes or until the crust is golden brown. Serve warm with mustard.

Potato Knishes

Makes 30 to 35 knishes

This is one of the official staple foods of New York City. They're sold everywhere: in ancient shops, at "kosher-style" delis, and even from street-corner pushcarts.

FILLING

"Potato Pierogi," page 159

WRAPPERS

"Knish Wrappers," page 170

Kasha Knishes

Makes 25 to 30 knishes

Long before there were potatoes in Eastern Europe, kasha was a staple. Made from buckwheat and with a great roasted flavor, this could well be the primal knish.

FILLING

1 tablespoon peanut oil

1/2 cup chopped onion
(about 1 small onion)

1 cup whole roasted kasha

2 1/2 cups chicken or vegetable broth

1/2 teaspoon salt

1/2 teaspoon freshly ground black pepper

WRAPPERS

"Knish Wrappers," page 170

To make the dumplings, see "Filling, Folding, and Cooking Knishes," page 171.

1. Heat the oil in a skillet over medium heat. Add the onion, and cook and stir for about 5 minutes or until the onions turn golden at the edges. Mix in the kasha, and cook until it's completely coated with the oil-onion mixture. Add the broth, salt, and pepper, turn up the heat, and bring the mixture to a boil. Let it boil for 2 minutes, reduce to a simmer, and then cover and cook for about 20 minutes or until all the liquid is absorbed. When the filling mixture is done, remove from the heat, set it aside, and let cool.

2. To make the dumplings, see "Filling, Folding, and Cooking Knishes," page 171.

Why Are They So Big?

During the research for this chapter, I really started wondering why it was that so many foods grew in size when they came to the United States. I already knew answers like "Americans like everything big" and "It's a big country," but they didn't satisfy. I wanted to know why immigrants who lived in late 19th-century urban America ate big food.

It didn't take long to get a much more credible answer. Back then, most people in these communities worked very long hours with few breaks; therefore, they'd need to find something that quickly filled them up—hence the giant knish or sandwich. It was enough to keep them going for five or six hours, until the next break. In addition, workers were forbidden to eat on the job, so when they finished, what they dreamed of—and got—was a giant plate of food.

For better or worse, this became part of "America." It was a response to a situation that sounds awful now but was a real improvement over what most of these people had left behind. It's something to remember the next time you groan at the sight of a huge portion.

Cabbage Knishes

Makes 25 to 30 knishes

Who even hears of cabbage as a knish filling these days? Potato is the standard and kasha a distant second, but a hundred years ago, cabbage was a common ingredient. Today it's as inexpensive and healthy as ever and worth a try.

FILLING

1 tablespoon peanut oil

1 cup chopped onion
(about 1 medium onion)

4 cups chopped or shredded cabbage
(about 1 small head; see note)

1 teaspoon caraway seeds

1 tablespoon chopped fresh dill

1 tablespoon cider vinegar

1/2 teaspoon salt

1/4 teaspoon freshly ground pepper

NOTE: Savoy cabbage is a good choice here, but at Yonnah Shimmel's Knishery on the Lower East Side of Manhattan, they use red with great success.

WRAPPERS

"Knish Wrappers," page 170

1. Heat the oil in a skillet over medium heat. Add the onions, and cook and stir for about 5 minutes or until the onions turn golden at the edges. Add the cabbage, caraway seeds, dill, vinegar, salt, and pepper, and continue cooking for about 10 minutes or until the cabbage has wilted completely, and the ingredients are evenly distributed. When the filling mixture is done, remove from the heat, set it aside, and let cool.

2. To make the dumplings, see "Filling, Folding, and Cooking Knishes," page 171.

Variation:
Add 1 or 2 cups chopped mushrooms along with the cabbage for a cabbage and mushroom knish.

The Perfect Cheap Date Restaurant for the Over-70 Crowd

If you were paying attention to the couple, you'd have noticed that he clearly behaved like a man who had convinced a woman that he was somehow worthwhile. She did little but lavish him with a glowing look of adoration and affirm his every word. When I was seated next to them, I was privately delighted to have the chance to eavesdrop.

Of course, the conversation turned out to be a continuous stream of complaints: the food wasn't as good as it was the first time, the soup was watery, the selections were strange. . . . Based on the way they were looking at each other, this was flirting and romance for the over-70 set.

I was visiting The Original Yonah Schimmel Knishery on East Houston Street in Manhattan, researching that classic of filled, baked dumplings: the knish. The place—with its vintage furniture and fixtures—really was original, but it was also "the remaining." Few other shops of this once-common genre were still in business. Mrs. Stahl's, the last remaining competitor in Brooklyn, had closed its doors five months earlier. The Knish-Nosh, though, was still there out on Queens Boulevard, in a neighborhood now infused by recent Jewish immigrants from Central Asia (see "Is There Really A Little Uzbekistan?" on page 102).

Here at Yonah Schimmel were knish varieties mentioned in memoirs of old New York but not seen since Elvis was a teenager: cabbage, kasha, and cherry—everything but liver. Of course, there was potato; it's the only variety most people remember, the survivor of the breed. Newcomers like spinach and sweet potato rounded out the menu.

Soon I had more than I bargained for. The happy, complaining couple was asking my opinion and trying to drag me into their conversation. "This place isn't as good as it was 60 years ago," the guy announced as a sort of a dare. The woman declared, "You used to be able to stand a spoon up in the soup."

Why, I thought, *would anybody want to stand a spoon up in their soup?*

The guy continued his litany of complaints while the woman gazed dreamily into his eyes. I was torn. Did I want to talk to these angry folks, or learn something about knishes?

Two were placed in front of me, each on its own saucer. The kasha knish was the color of dark wood and had a scent that was almost like roasting coffee. And the cabbage was . . . um . . . well, the color of red cabbage and had a tang of vinegar when I bit into it.

The couple paid and left, and when I looked over at their table, I saw that much of their food was uneaten. I wanted to feel sad about this, but my own two knishes were so delicious and so obviously handcrafted that I couldn't sink into the deep funk that I somehow felt was appropriate.

Soon the manager was talking to me. He had a whole theory about how the departed couple had just been trying to show how much they knew. I wanted him to talk about knishes, and I managed to get a story out of him. He told me how they started using red cabbage instead of green. It began when a vegetable supplier shipped him red by mistake. When the cook saw it, she thought it was worth a try, and it turned out to offer two advantages; first, it tasted better, and second, the bright-red shreds of cabbage looked nothing like any other filling, reducing the possibility of error on busy days.

I thought the red-cabbage knish was delicious. It was a happy mistake—or at least a mistake that made *me* happy.

WESTERN
EUROPE

Maulaschenin in Broth

German Stuffed Pasta in Soup (Maultaschen)

Makes 36 dumplings (6 servings)

Now we're in the heart of Western Europe, and we're starting to see ravioli. What makes them different? Well, instead of folding, two layers of dough are rolled out separately and sealed together at the edges. Maultaschen—which are like large ravioli—may be made with an Italian method, but served in beef broth or with onions, they become German through and through.

1. Combine the beef, bread crumbs, spinach, salt, pepper, nutmeg, allspice, parsley and egg in a large bowl. Mix well—your hands are great for this—and make sure that all the ingredients are evenly distributed. Refrigerate for 30 minutes so that the flavors can combine and the bread crumbs can absorb the moisture.

2. To form each maultaschen, you'll need 2 squares of pasta and 1 1/2 teaspoons of filling. Place the filling in the center of the bottom square, lay the top over it and press the edges to seal, pressing the air out from the inside as you go along.

3. Bring the salted water to a boil in a large pot. Add the filled dumplings to the boiling water using a slotted spoon or wire basket, return the water to a boil, reduce the heat, and simmer for about 10 minutes or until the meat is completely cooked (see "Make the Sacrifice" in "Basics"), stirring occasionally to make sure that the dumplings don't stick to the pot but not so much that they burst. Remove with the same utensil you used to put them in, and drain.

4. Heat the beef broth. For each serving, put a cup of warm soup in a bowl, and place six of the cooked and drained maultaschen. Garnish each bowl with some of the remaining parsley, and serve immediately.

Variation:
Another way to serve maultaschen is to put the drained dumplings on a plate and top with a bit of melted butter. Add some caramelized onions (see page 161) on the side.

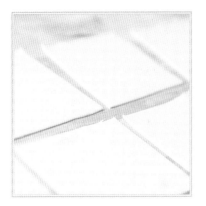

FILLING

1/2 pound ground beef

1 cup unseasoned bread crumbs

1 package (10 ounces) frozen, chopped
    spinach, thawed and drained

1/2 teaspoon salt

1/4 teaspoon freshly ground pepper

1/2 teaspoon ground nutmeg

1/4 teaspoon ground allspice

2 tablespoons finely chopped parsley
    plus 2 tablespoons for garnish

1 egg

WRAPPERS

2 recipes "Kreplach Wrappers," page 164,
    cut into 3 inch squares or

1 recipe "Egg- and Dairy-Free Pierogi
    Wrappers," page 153

6 quarts salted water

SOUP

1 quart beef broth

Cooked Potato

Swedish Potato and Bacon Dumplings (Kroppkakor)

Makes 8 dumplings

When I asked a Swedish friend about these, he told me to imagine giant gnocchi with filling inside. No sheets of dough are rolled out for kroppkakor; instead, you poke a hole in a ball of dough, push in the filling, and then plug the opening. It's just one more variation on the filled dumpling theme.

1. Heat the bacon, onion, allspice, and pepper in a skillet over medium heat. Cook and stir until the bacon is golden brown and the onions are browning at the edges. When the filling mixture is done, remove from the heat, set it aside, and let cool.

2. Combine the potato, flour, egg, the teaspoon of salt, and 1/4 cup water in a large bowl, and knead until a dough forms. If the dough is dry and cracking, add more water 1 tablespoon at a time until it's moist and springy and you have a mixture with the same consistency as Play Doh™. If the dough is sticky, add more flour 1 tablespoon at a time until it's smooth. Knead the dough for about 5 more minutes or until a poke with a finger will bounce back like a soft pillow. Cover the dough with plastic wrap, and let it rest for 30 minutes.

3. Form the dough into 8 balls, each roughly 2 1/2 inches in diameter—about the size of a small onion. Holding a ball in the palm of

FILLING

2 cups chopped bacon (about 8 ounces)

1 cup chopped onion (about 1 large onion)

1/2 teaspoon ground allspice

1/2 teaspoon freshly ground pepper

WRAPPERS

4 cups potatoes, cooked, peeled, and mashed (about 3 large potatoes)

1 cup all-purpose flour

1 egg

1 teaspoon salt plus salt for the cooking water

1/4 cup water

6 quarts water for cooking

your hand, poke a hole in it with the index finger of your other hand. The hole should go to the center of the ball, but not deeper. Spoon 1 teaspoon of filling into the hole, and seal it with your fingers.

4. Bring of the cooking water to a boil, add the kroppkakor with a slotted spoon or wire basket. Return it to a boil, and then reduce the heat to a simmer. Cook the dumplings for 11 minutes or until they're hot in the center, and remove them with the same utensil you used to put them in. Drain. Serve immediately.

5. Kroppkakor are most often served hot with butter and berry jam. Traditional Swedish flavors like lingonberry are the first choice, but any red berry jam will do in a pinch.

Tortellini

Ravioli

For many of us, these are the dumplings that define Italian food and the ones we eat most often. In fine Italian restaurants where they're filled with wild mushrooms, in school lunchrooms where they're filled with ground meat, from your supermarket's freezer where they're filled with spinach, or even from a can where they're already swimming in tomato sauce, ravioli are an everyday food.

Italian-Style Pasta Wrappers

Makes wrappers for 50 medium-sized ravioli

Since Italian chefs consider their dumplings to be treasures, it's only fitting that their dough be the richest in the book.

1 1/2 cups all-purpose flour

1 1/2 cups semolina flour

1/2 teaspoon salt

4 large eggs

2 tablespoons olive oil

2 tablespoons water

1. Sift the flours and salt together, and then mound them into the shape of a volcano with a crater—most of us will do this in a large bowl, but the truly courageous will make it on a flat surface. Pour the eggs, oil, and water into the crater, and, using a fork, take small bits of flour from the outside edge of the crater, add to the center, and stir into the egg/oil mixture. When the dough becomes too thick to work with the fork, start kneading for about 3 or 4 minutes or until it's elastic. Cover the dough with plastic wrap, and refrigerate for at least 30 minutes. If need be, it can stay refrigerated for several hours.

2. Divide the dough into quarters, and press each piece flat with your hand. Use a pasta machine (see "Pasta Machine 101" in "Basics"), and crank the sheets through until you have a thin dough—number 5 on my machine. The wrappers are now ready to be filled and cooked.

White Wine Pasta Wrappers

Makes wrappers for 48 large ravioli

When I visited the kitchen at Tre Piani Restaurant (see page 198), I was hoping to see them make their white-wine pasta dough. It didn't happen, though—the recipe was just too easy. They said, "All we do is just mix flour and white wine, and then knead it into a dough." Here's my version.

1. Combine the flour, salt and wine in a large bowl, and mix them together with a spoon until a dough begins to form. If the dough is dry and cracking, add more wine 1 tablespoon at a time until it's moist and springy; if the dough is sticky, add more flour 1 tablespoon at a time until it's smooth. On a floured surface, knead the dough for about 2 or 3 minutes or until it's elastic. Cover the dough with plastic wrap and refrigerate for at least 30 minutes. If need be, it can stay refrigerated for several hours.

2. Divide the dough into quarters and press each piece flat. Use a pasta machine (see "Pasta Machine 101" in "Basics"), and crank the sheets through until you create moderately a thin dough—number 5 on my machine. The wrappers are now ready to be filled and cooked.

3 cups unbleached all-purpose flour

1/2 teaspoon salt

1 1/4 cups dry white wine (Any dry, white table wine will work: leftovers from a previous night's dinner, that bargain bottle from a discount store, or anything that's on hand. If it's not "off," it will do the job.)

Filling, Forming, and Cooking Ravioli

1. To form the ravioli, lay out a sheet of pasta (see "Italian Style Pasta Dough" on page 186 or "White Wine Pasta Wrappers" on page 187), and put a 1/2 teaspoon of filling in rows 2 inches apart on it. Then lay a second sheet of pasta on top; using your hands, press down around each little ball of filling to get the air out and encourage the two layers of pasta to stick and form a sealed pocket. Next, separate the ravioli using either a cutting wheel (to form squares) or a stamp made for the purpose (for round or other shapes). Lay the individual ravioli out on a cookie sheet covered with parchment paper. They can also be frozen at this point.

2. To make smaller ravioli, you'll find it easiest with a mold. Lay the mold down on a flat surface and place a sheet of rolled-out pasta over it. Gently press and stretch the pasta into the wells. Then spoon the filling into the wells, and cover the whole mold with another sheet of pasta. Now use a rolling pin to press the top sheet of pasta into the mold, sealing and separating each of the ravioli. You may need a small paring knife to help remove and separate them.

3. Cook the ravioli by bringing 6 quarts of salted water to a boil in a large pot. Use a slotted spoon or wire basket to add the filled ravioli to the boiling water, return the water to a boil, reduce to a simmer, and cook for about 7 minutes or until the dough is completely done. Stir the ravioli every now and then to make sure they don't stick to the pot but not so much that they burst. Drain and serve.

Beef Ravioli

Makes 48 medium-sized ravioli (about 4 servings)

Some people always seem to have leftovers hanging around. Their fridges are filled with partially eaten roast chickens, containers of Chinese takeout, and perhaps even the remnants of fancy dinner parties. For them this dish will be a breeze; for the rest of us, finding a bit of cold pot roast might be a challenge (I used roast beef from a deli with good results). Give them a try, though; their deep flavor is worth the effort.

1. Combine the beef, ricotta, Parmesan, parsley, salt, and pepper in a large bowl, and mix until all the ingredients are well blended. If you're not going to fill the wrappers immediately, refrigerate the mixture until ready.

2. To make the dumplings, see "Forming, Filling, and Cooking Ravioli," page 188. 3. Serve with Simple Tomato Sauce (see page 212) or with a dash of olive oil, a chopped fresh sage leaf, and a tablespoon of grated cheese.

FILLING

1 1/2 cups finely chopped cold pot roast
or roast beef (about 1/2 pound)

1 cup ricotta cheese

1/4 cup grated Parmesan cheese

1/2 cup finely chopped Italian parsley

1/2 teaspoon salt

1/4 teaspoon freshly ground pepper

WRAPPERS

"Italian-Style Pasta Dough," page 186

Cheese, Raisin, and Rum Ravioli (Krafi)

Makes 50 ravioli

They call these "Wedding Ravioli" in Istria, the Italian region they come from. You don't have to wait for a wedding, though. Krafi are great for any special occasion.

FILLING

1 cup golden raisins or sultanas

1/2 cup rum

1 egg

1 teaspoon sugar

1 cup shredded fontal or
       Italian Fontina cheese
       (about 8 ounces)

1/2 cup grated Parmesan cheese
       plus extra for topping

1/2 cup unseasoned dry breadcrumbs

2 tablespoons grated lemon zest

1/4 cup grated orange zest

Melted butter for topping

WRAPPERS

"Pasta Dough Made with White Wine,"
       page 187

1. Soak the raisins in the rum for at least 1 hour or until they're plump. Drain and set aside.

2. Combine the egg and sugar in a bowl, and whisk them together until the sugar is dissolved. Mix in the cheeses, breadcrumbs, and lemon and orange zests, making sure that all the ingredients are well distributed. If you're not going to fill the wrappers immediately, refrigerate the mixture until ready.

3. To make the dumplings, see "Forming, Filling, and Cooking Ravioli," page 188. If you're using a mold, choose a large one; this won't work if there's just one lonely raisin in each dumpling.

4. Serve the ravioli with the melted butter and a bit more grated Parmesan cheese.

In Italy, the Tools of the Trade

In Italy, people eat an awful lot of dumplings. Ravioli, tortellini, and panzerotti are each considered genres, not foods. Eating there is always a revelation, but on a recent trip I started wondering about another aspect of Italian dumpling culture: the tools of the trade.

At a supermarket, it took me more than a few minutes to get by the huge displays of fresh and frozen stuffed pastas. Some ravioli were as small as a thumbnail and others were so big that one could almost fill a plate. Tortellini were available—both fresh and frozen—in huge, economy-sized sacks that could feed an extended family for a month. Of course, in tradition-bound Italy, there were no surprises in the fillings department: Beef, ham and ricotta, spinach, mushroom, and four cheese were the mainstays.

I wasn't settling for premade, though, and was soon in the housewares section. It was filled with the sorts of tools Americans can only find in specialized stores. You know, the ones in upscale malls that also sell $7 packages of unpopped popcorn and 18 different fruit mustards.

First I found a great set of dumpling presses. Three different sizes were packed together. Even though I own five already, I bought more. The biggest was typical of what's sold in Asian markets back home, but the two smaller sizes were unique. Then there were roller/cutters, both with and without crimpers—perfect for ravioli. Finally, a great selection of rolling pins, from

tiny to ones big enough to mug an elephant, but I passed on them. It was one part of the kitchen where I was already well-equipped.

At a large appliance store, I expected—but didn't find—electric pasta machines, but I did see a wide variety of deep fryers. These would make dishes like panzerotti (see page 207) far easier and, thanks to their automatic temperature controls, much more repeatable.

All that was missing were those flat ravioli molds you occasionally see on TV. In the small northern city of Cuneo, I visited the most elegant kitchen-supply store I had ever seen (I could almost imagine it having a velvet rope and a bouncer out front). Inside, there were $17 slotted spoons and $80 coffeepots—but no molds. I asked—and got a giggle in response. For those, I needed to go to the cheap store down the street and up a back alley. There, among the replacement drain stoppers and colorful plastic clothespins, I found the ravioli molds waiting for me.

Ravioli? Tortellini? Panzerotti? Back home, with my gear stash at hand, I was ready.

Asparagus and Mushroom Ravioli

Makes 48 medium-sized ravioli (about 4 servings)

With two strong flavors, asparagus and mushrooms, this is a great vegetarian choice. If you use "Pasta Dough Made with White Wine" on page 187 for the wrappers, the recipe becomes vegan.

1. Heat the oil in a skillet over medium heat. Add the garlic and oregano, and cook and stir for about 5 minutes or until the edges of the garlic brown a bit. Add the mushrooms, asparagus, salt, and pepper, and continue cooking, occasionally stirring, for about 20 minutes more or until the mushrooms are well browned and the asparagus is fully cooked..

2. To make the dumplings, see "Forming, Filling, and Cooking Ravioli," page 188.

3. Serve topped with butter and garnished with a spoonful of grated Parmesan cheese and a couple of fresh sage leaves.

FILLING

1 tablespoon olive oil

2 cloves garlic, finely chopped

1/2 teaspoon dried oregano

2 cups finely chopped mushrooms (about one 8-ounce package)

2 cups chopped fresh asparagus

1/2 teaspoon salt

1/4 teaspoon freshly ground pepper

WRAPPERS

"Italian-Style Pasta Dough," page 186 or "Pasta Dough Made with White Wine," page 187

TOPPING

Butter

Garnish

Parmesan cheese

Fresh sage leaves

Ravioli Filled with Turkey and Pancetta

Makes 48 medium-sized ravioli
(about 4 servings)

This is based on a recipe that uses leftovers turkey, but in my house, we never have any. So I had to come up with something else (or we'd never eat it). Sliced turkey breast sold at supermarkets did the job perfectly.

FILLING

1/2 cup finely chopped pancetta (see note)

1 1/2 cups finely chopped roast turkey meat

1 cup ricotta cheese

2 tablespoons grated Parmesan cheese

1/2 teaspoon dried rosemary

1/2 teaspoon dried oregano

1/4 teaspoon salt

1/4 teaspoon freshly ground pepper

WRAPPERS

"Italian-Style Pasta Dough," page 186

SAUCE

"Simple Tomato Sauce," page 212

GARNISH

Grated Parmesan cheese

Chili flakes

NOTE: While pancetta is often called "Italian bacon," don't substitute bacon here. Pancetta needs no further cooking, making it a fine match for the precooked turkey.

1. Combine the pancetta, turkey, ricotta, Parmesan, rosemary, oregano, salt, and pepper in a large bowl, and mix (your hands work well here) until all the ingredients are well combined and evenly distributed.

2. To make the dumplings, see "Filling, Forming, and Cooking Ravioli," page 188.

3. Serve with "Simple Tomato Sauce," page 212, garnished with a bit more grated cheese and dried chili flakes.

Squash and Amaretti Ravioli

Makes 48 medium-sized ravioli (about 4 servings)

Not so long ago, squash fillings were exotic, but these days they're showing up on menus and even in freezer cases all over the place.

1. Combine the squash, crushed cookies, ricotta, raisins, egg, nutmeg, salt, and pepper in a large bowl, and mix (your hands work well here) until all the ingredients are well combined and evenly distributed. If you're not going to fill the wrappers immediately, refrigerate the mixture until ready.

2. To make the dumplings, see "Filling, Forming, and Cooking Ravioli," page 188.

3. Serve topped with melted butter garnished with a spoonful of grated Parmesan cheese.

FILLING

1 1/2 cups mashed, cooked squash (or one 12-ounce package frozen cooked winter squash)

1 cup crushed Amaretti cookies

1 cup ricotta cheese

1/2 cup chopped raisins

1 egg

1/2 teaspoon ground nutmeg

1/2 teaspoon salt

1/4 teaspoon freshly ground pepper

WRAPPERS

"Italian-Style Pasta Dough," page 186

TOPPING

Melted butter

Grated Parmesan cheese

Rice and Cabbage Ravioli

Makes 48 medium-sized ravioli (about 4 servings)

Italian chefs are the greatest recyclers in the food universe. Nothing that's still edible is ever thrown away. A leftover roast can have its juices used as a sauce for pasta and the meat made into filling. But it isn't just meat that's repurposed; in this recipe, cooked rice is the ingredient. Combined with the staples of cabbage, hard cheese, and butter, and then stuffed into ravioli, we have everyday ingredients turned into something completely new.

1. Melt the butter in a heavy skillet over medium heat. Add the cabbage, and cook and stir for about 20 minutes or until the cabbage is completely wilted and the edges turn golden. Mix in the rice, cheese, salt, and pepper, and continue cooking until all the ingredients are well combined and evenly distributed. When the filling mixture is done, remove from the heat, set it aside, and let cool. If you're not going to fill the wrappers immediately, refrigerate the mixture until ready.

2. To make the dumplings, see "Filling, Forming, and Cooking Ravioli," page 188.

3. Serve with melted butter garnished with a spoonful of grated Parmesan cheese and a couple of fresh sage leaves.

FILLING

1 tablespoon butter

2 cups shredded Savoy cabbage

2 cups cooked rice (see note)

1/2 cup grated Parmesan cheese

1/2 teaspoon salt

1/4 teaspoon freshly ground pepper

NOTE: An Italian rice like arborio works best, but even the rice from a Chinese takeout shop will do just fine.

WRAPPERS

"Italian-Style Pasta Dough," page 186

TOPPING

Melted butter

GARNISH

Parmesan cheese

Fresh sage leaves

In the Kitchen at Tre Piani

Most of the time we think of dumplings as snack food—
something cheap you can grab on the run. The street
vendors in Flushing, Queens, and Brighton Beach,
Brooklyn, set the tone for much of this book: Dumplings
are a poor person's food—or at least a rushed person's.
It's not always that way, though; there are those Beggar's
Purses (see page 136) that have hints of Czarist luxury.
But in my opinion, the most elevated role you'll find
the dumpling playing is in the pasta course of a fine
Italian meal.

After a year of what might be best described
as "intensive snack research," I though I had better go
see an expert. Chef Jim Weaver of Tre Piani Restaurant
in Princeton, New Jersey, was just such a person; his is
one of the best fine-dining Italian restaurants in intensely
Italian Central New Jersey, and he was famed for his
pasta-making skills. I visited Jim in his kitchen at three
o'clock on a Tuesday afternoon. Restaurant people
would call this a slow time on a slow day, but to an
outsider, it was still a madhouse.

I had hoped that Jim would make his "silk"
pasta—a wrapper dough made with just flour and white
wine. It didn't happen, though. (You'll find the recipe
on page 187, anyway.) The ingredients Jim had that
day—sheep's-milk ricotta, homemade lamb sausage,
and good fresh artichokes—inspired him to make
something entirely different.

Whatever the recipe, it was the technique that

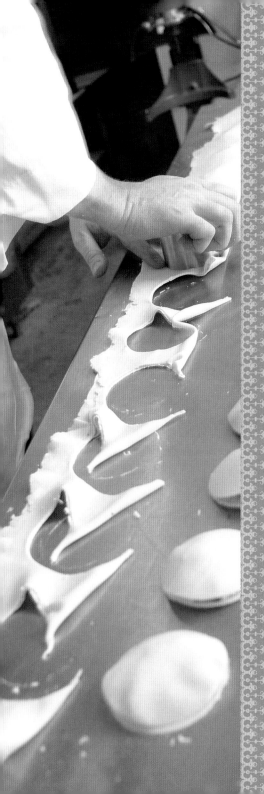

hypnotized me. Jim was doing things that Italian home cooks didn't do. When he made the wrapper dough, he kneaded it far less than most people and ran it through the pasta machine far more often. This, he told me, did a better job of developing texture. Back in my own kitchen, I tried it with "Italian-Style Pasta Dough" (page 186) and "Egg- and Dairy-Free Pierogi Wrappers" (page 153). Both improved greatly; all the mushiness was gone, and they had a real chew without any feeling of being undercooked.

Chef Weaver's filling and sauce were no less impressive. For the filling he used a local sheep's milk ricotta, and for a sauce, house-made lamb sausage and artichokes. It appeared on that night's menu as "Homemade Sheep's Milk Ricotta Ravioli Served with a Ragu of Lamb Sausage, Fresh Artichoke Hearts, Tomatoes, and Peas."

Jim and I sampled the dish in a relatively quiet corner of the kitchen. "These are very Roman flavors," he told me. I thought he meant the perfect chewy texture of his pasta, but he was referring to the lamb, peas, and artichokes. Still, it was that chewiness that caught me. Italians call it *al dente,* meaning "at teeth," and all too often Americans misdefine al dente as "undercooked." These ravioli were cooked perfectly though and so full of flavor that I needed more than a few bites to get a grasp on everything that was there.

Back home, I pondered the experience. Yes, there were incredible ingredients. Yes, this guy had lots of experience and was willing to put in huge amounts of time to get things right. But in the end, it was the al dente that got me. The resistance the pasta offered without being tough; the way it made me understand how too much of what I'd been eating in the past was just plain mushy. It was a lesson in technique that I was able to put to work the very next day.

Small Italian Dumplings (Tortellini)

We saw our first bowl of dumplings in soup over 5,000 miles east of here, and the style of serving is still going strong. But here's where the combination—and the Silk Road itself—come to an end. No matter how hard you look, you're unlikely to see a Cornish pasty (see page 217) or an empanada (see page 239) served in broth. Like all sorts of other dishes that Americans call "Italian," tortellini names and recipes vary greatly in their country of origin. "Cappelletti" and "umbelichi sacri" (yes, "sacred navels") are other names for tortellini. "Cappellacci" and "tortelloni" are just big tortellini.

Filling, Forming, and Cooking Tortellini

Tortellini, cappelletti, and their relatives are folded in roughly the same way as vushka (see page 148), with one difference: You put a finger in the middle when folding them across so there's a bit of space. This lets the cooking water reach the inside faster.

1. Begin with small disks of rolled-out pasta dough (a 2-inch round cookie-cutter does the job well), spoon a tiny bit of filling on top, fold into a half-moon shape, and then—with your index finger across the middle—fold them in half again. Yes, they look elaborate, but that's all there is to it.

2. Offically, use 1/4 teaspoon of filling per tortellini. Remember: The amount of filling is minuscule; it's all about the dough. Use something like a demitasse spoon (those little ones that accopany cups of espresso) so that you can get tiny, but consistent amounts of filling on the dough disks. Put a bit of filling in the center of the disks.

3. Fold the disk of dough in half, press the air out and seal the edges. Fold the tortellini once again, this time over your index finger in order to allow some space for water to flow through and properly cook the whole thing.

Ricotta and Herb Tortellini

Makes 100 tortellini

If you study Italian pasta fillings for any length of time, you'll start to see a pattern. Ricotta is the base, and everything else is just mixed in. This can get you wondering: If you have a good ricotta, how much more do you really need? Salt? Pepper? Some herbs?

1. Combine the ricotta, salt, pepper, thyme, and sage in a large bowl, and mix thoroughly to make sure that all the herbs are well distributed. Refrigerate the filling mixture for at least 1 hour so that the flavors can blend.

2. To make the dumplings, see "Filling, Forming, and Cooking Tortellini," page 200.

3. Serve with butter and a bit of grated Parmesan cheese or in broth (see page 205).

FILLING

2 cups ricotta cheese

1/2 teaspoon salt

1/4 teaspoon freshly ground pepper (see note)

1 tablespoon finely chopped fresh thyme

1 tablespoon finely chopped fresh sage

NOTE: Use white pepper if you can; black will look like dirt against the white background

WRAPPERS

"Italian-Style Pasta Dough," page 186, or "White-Wine Pasta Dough," 187

TOPPING

Butter

Grated Parmesan cheese

Four Cheese Tortellini

Makes 100 Tortellini

Four-cheese tortellini seems to be on lots of menus, but no two seem to be able to agree on which four cheeses belong. Ricotta seems to go in every cheese-based filling. Now we need three more. How about a good blue like Gorgonzola, a creamy fontal or fontina, and a sharp, spicy pecorino?

FILLING

1 cup ricotta cheese

1/2 cup finely crumbled Gorgonzola cheese (about 3 ounces; see note)

1/2 cup shredded fontal cheese

1/4 cup grated Pecorino Romano

1/2 teaspoon ground nutmeg

1/2 teaspoon salt

1/4 teaspoon freshly ground pepper

NOTE: Use any fresh blue cheese if you can't find this one.

WRAPPERS

"Italian-Style Pasta Dough," page 186, or "White-Wine Pasta Dough," 187

TOPPING

Butter

Grated Parmesan cheese

1. Combine the ricotta, Gorgonzola, fontal, pecorino, nutmeg, salt, and pepper in a bowl and mix thoroughly; you might need a potato masher or similar tool to achieve this. Refrigerate the filling mixture for at least 1 hour so that the flavors can blend.

2. To make the dumplings, see "Filling, Forming, and Cooking Tortellini," page 200.

3. Serve with butter and a bit of grated Parmesan cheese or in broth (see page 205).

Shrimp Tortellini

Makes 100 Tortellini

Shrimp are somewhere between everyday and luxury: above beef or pork and a bit beneath lobster or wild mushrooms. Does that make this filling right for a special occasion? Maybe—or it might be what makes a dinner special.

1. Combine the shrimp, egg, parsley, salt, and pepper, and mix thoroughly. Because this filling uses raw, fresh seafood, you'll have to move quickly. Refrigerate the filling mixture as soon as you've made it, and return it there when you're not filling the dough.

2. To make the dumplings, see "Filling, Forming, and Cooking Tortellini," page 200.

3. Serve with a bit of butter or tomato sauce.

FILLING

2 cups finely chopped shelled, deveined shrimp meat (about 12 ounces)

1 lightly beaten egg

2 tablespoons finely chopped Italian parsley

1/2 teaspoon salt

1/4 teaspoon freshly ground pepper

WRAPPERS

"Italian-Style Pasta Dough," page 186, or "White-Wine Pasta Dough," 187

TOPPING

Butter or "Simple Tomato Sauce," page 212

Spinach Tortellini

Makes 100 Tortellini

Spinach-filled pastas are everywhere. Once considered exotic, they morphed into vegetarian alternatives and today's typical varieties.

FILLING

1 package (10 ounces) frozen, chopped spinach, thawed and drained

1 cup ricotta cheese

2 tablespoons grated Parmesan cheese

1/2 teaspoon ground nutmeg

1/2 teaspoon salt

1/4 teaspoon freshly ground pepper

WRAPPERS

"Italian-Style Pasta Dough," page 186, or "White-Wine Pasta Dough," 187

TOPPING

Butter

Grated Parmesan cheese or

"Simple Tomato Sauce," page 212

1. Combine the spinach, ricotta, Parmesan, nutmeg, salt, and pepper in a bowl, and mix thoroughly, making sure that all the ingredients are well distributed. Your hands do the best job here. Refrigerate for at least 30 minutes so that the flavors can blend.

2. To make the dumplings, see "Filling, Forming, and Cooking Tortellini," page 200.

3. Serve with a bit of butter and grated Parmesan cheese or tomato sauce.

Tortellini in Broth (Tortellini in Brodo)

Makes 4 servings

"Dumplings in soup" Where have we heard that before? The details always seem to differ. In China, wontons are served in chicken broth; in Eastern Europe, vushka are offered in bright-red borscht; and in Italy, people pair tortellini with beef broth.

1. Bring the broth to a boil in a large pot, and add the tortellini using a slotted spoon or wire basket. Return the water to a boil, lower the heat to a simmer, and cook and stir for about 7 minutes or until the pasta and filling are completely cooked (see "Make the Sacrifice" in "Basics").

2. To serve, ladle the soup and tortellini into bowls, making sure that everybody gets the exact same amount (to avoid those inevitable arguments). Sprinkle with grated cheese at the table.

4 cups beef broth

40 uncooked, filled tortellini (see note)

4 tablespoons grated Parmesan cheese

NOTE: You can use any filling except shrimp, which doesn't seem to go with beef broth.

Broth, Bullion Cubes, Stock

For me, the biggest problem in making dishes like "Tortellini in Brodo" is the soup. If you happened to have made a classic Italian boiled-beef dish the day before, you'll have enough broth left over. And if you're lucky, you'll have enough cooked meat to use in a filling, too. The rest of us will have to look elsewhere.

A tour of local food markets came up with a variety of possibilities: containers, concentrates, and cubes. Let's take them one at a time.

Containers of ready-to-use broth come in both cans and cartons. While none of the brands I tried had strong or "off" flavors, some were more salty than others. My best results were with low-sodium varieties. You should also note that while some of these products are labeled "stock" and others "broth," their tastes were quite similar.

Concentrates—pastes meant to be diluted with water—had decent, sometimes good, flavor when mixed correctly but were a disaster if mismeasured. Be careful here!

Bullion cubes are called "dadi" (dice) in Italian, and no word could more perfectly describe my experiences; both the best and worst prepared broths I've had came from them. Be aware that even the same brand and variety can have very different flavors when bought in different stores; a cube from a global company will have a flavor tailored to the market of the language printed on the package. So those Spanish, Polish, or Chinese boxes you've seen differ in more ways than you think.

My recommendation? Try Italian bullion cubes if you can find them and other European or South American varieties as a second choice. Asian brands are often excellent but have seasonings like soy sauce that will clash with western flavors. If all you have is the local supermarket, try low-sodium broth or stock in the container. None of the brands I tried were great—but, then again, none were awful, either.

By the way, technically speaking; "stock" comes from bones and broth from meat. But there's also vegetable stock. . . .

Italian Fried Dumplings (Panzerotti)

When we're discussing Italian cuisine, most of us don't think of fried food. But while deep frying doesn't have a long, national tradition, there are places where fried snacks are part of daily life. Panzerotti—fried Italian dumplings—are a perfect example.

Legend has it that panzerotti began as deep-fried ravioli, but evolution has changed things a bit. Today they are almost always half-moon shaped and use the same yeast-raised dough as pizza and calzones.

Panzerotti Wrappers

Makes 40 wrappers

This is a dough that anybody who's made a pizza from scratch would be familiar with: yeast, something to get that yeast going, flour, olive oil (always!), and a bit of salt. Remember that even though the wrappers are rolled thin, the ingredients give a distinct texture and flavor.

1 cup water (see note)

1/2 teaspoon sugar

1 packet active dry yeast

2 cups unbleached white flour plus flour
        for work surface

2 tablespoons olive oil

1/2 teaspoon salt

Canola oil or canola oil spray for
        the rising bowl

NOTE: I find that I get much better results using bottled water because the chlorine in my tap water kills the yeast before it can rise.

1. Warm the water to about 100 degrees, and mix in the sugar and yeast. Let stand at room temperature for about 10 minutes or until the yeast begins to bubble and froth.

2. Combine the yeast liquid, flour, oil, and salt in a large bowl, and mix until a thick dough forms. On a well-floured work surface, knead the dough for about 7 minutes or until it's elastic. Put the dough in a well-oiled bowl, cover it with a towel, and let it rest for 3 hours or until it doubles in size. Divide the dough into 6 equal pieces, flatten them a bit with your palm and roll the dough out into thin sheets using a pasta machine (see "Pasta Machine 101" in "Basics"). It will take a few more passes than normal, but the result will be a tender wrapper that's perfect when fried. Cut the dough into 3-inch diameter disks (use a cookie cutter or a small bowl as a template). The wrappers are now ready to be filled and cooked.

Filling, Forming, and Cooking Panzerotti

Panzerotti are formed using the traditional "Half-Moon Method" (see "The Basics," page 25), and a dumpling press (see page 25) is a big help. Note that while some people say that you can bake panzerotti, my own opinion is that once you put them in the oven, they become calzones, a whole different animal.

1. Use a 3-inch diameter cookie-cutter to form disks of dough. Spoon a heaping teaspoon of filling into the center, fold the dough in half, and seal the edges.

2. To fry panzerotti, heat the oil in a heavy pot over medium or medium-high heat, and stir occasionally until the oil reaches 375 degrees. Gently lower the dumplings into the oil using a slotted spoon or wire basket. Continue cooking until the dumplings are golden brown. Remove from the oil using the same utensil you used to put them in. Drain on paper towels.

3. Serve panzerotti as a snack or appetizer.

Fresh Tomato and Mozzarella Panzerotti

Makes filling for 20 panzerotti

Tomato. Basil. Mozzarella. With a filling that almost reads like a dictionary of Italian basics, this is a good place to enter the panzerotti universe.

FILLING

1 1/2 cups shredded mozzarella cheese

1 cup chopped fresh tomato
    (about 1 medium tomato)

2 tablespoon grated Parmesan cheese

1 tablespoon finely chopped fresh basil

1/2 teaspoon dried oregano

1/2 teaspoon salt

1/2 teaspoon freshly ground pepper

WRAPPERS

"Panzerotti Wrappers," page 208

At least 3 quarts of peanut oil for frying

1. Combine the mozzarella, tomato, Parmesan, basil, oregano, salt, and pepper in a large bowl, making sure that all the ingredients are well distributed. If you're not going to fill the wrappers immediately, refrigerate the mixture until ready.

2. Follow the instructions for "Filling, Forming, and Cooking Panzerotti," page 209.

Chopped Anchovy, Salami, Caper, and Olive Panzerotti

Makes 20 panzerotti

Just like "Fresh Tomato and Mozzarella Panzerotti" (page 210), these have basic ingredients and rely on the blast of heat from deep frying to get their unique flavor and texture.

1. To make the filling, heat the olive oil in a skillet over medium heat. Add the anchovies, and cook and stir for about 1 minute or until the anchovies dissolve in the oil. Add the salami, and continue cooking for about 5 minutes or until the edges of the salami turn brown. Mix in the onion, capers, olives, parsley, cheese, salt, and pepper, and continue cooking and stirring for about 10 more minutes or until the onions have turned translucent. When the filling mixture is done, remove from the heat, set it aside, and let cool.

2. Follow the instructions for "Filling, Forming, and Cooking Panzerotti," page 209.

FILLING

1 tablespoon olive oil

4 anchovy fillets

1 cup chopped hard salami

1 cup chopped onion
    (about 1 medium onion)

2 tablespoons capers, rinsed and drained

1/2 cup chopped pitted olives (see note)

1/4 cup finely chopped fresh Italian parsley

2 tablespoons grated Parmesan cheese

1/2 teaspoon freshly ground black pepper

NOTE: Try to avoid olives that are canned and packed in brine. Many supermarkets and Middle Eastern groceries will have good-quality pitted olives for cooking.

WRAPPERS

"Panzerotti Wrappers," page 208

Side Dish: Simple Tomato Sauce

Makes 3 cups (for 4 servings of pasta)

It doesn't matter if you choose ravioli, tortellini, or any other pasta; the easiest way to turn it into a meal is with a simple (some people call it "basic") tomato sauce. The sauce is great with many of the Italian pastas here in the book. At the table, most people will sprinkle a spoonful of grated Parmesan cheese on top, and many will add a pinch of crushed red pepper, too.

SAUCE

1 tablespoon olive oil

1 teaspoon dried oregano

3 cloves garlic, chopped

1 can (28 ounces) crushed tomatoes

1/2 teaspoon salt, or to taste

1/4 teaspoon freshly ground black
        pepper, or to taste

3 fresh basil leaves

GARNISH

Grated Parmesan cheese

Crushed red pepper

1. Heat the olive oil in a pan over medium heat. Add the oregano and garlic, and cook and stir for about 10 minutes or until the edges of the garlic pieces turn golden. Stir in the tomatoes, lower the heat a bit, and continue cooking for about 20 minutes or until a quarter of the liquid evaporates. Sample the sauce, and add the salt and pepper to taste. The sauce is ready when the raw tomato flavor is gone.

2. Just before serving, tear the basil leaves into shreds and add them to the sauce.

Fast and Naked (Gnudi con Zucca)

Makes about 4 servings

Gnudi are typical ravioli or tortellini fillings enriched to the point where they need no wrappers. Also known as "Gnocchi Gnudi" or "Malfatti," they're what you want to make when you don't have the time to fill and fold. The name means "nudes" (because there's no pasta), and their reputation is as a dish that can be made quickly.

Gnudi are often flavored with spinach or chard, but this time I've chosen a more unusual variation: gnudi con zucca—gnudi with squash.

1. Combine the squash, ricotta, eggs, Parmesan, flour, nutmeg, sage, 1/2 teaspoon of salt, and pepper in a bowl, and mix until a dough forms. If the dough is too dry, add water 1 teaspoon at a time until it's moist; if the dough is too sticky, add more flour 1 teaspoon at a time until it's smooth. (A little bit makes a big difference.)

2. On a floured work surface, knead the dough for about 3 or 4 minutes or a poke with a finger will bounce back like a soft pillow. Divide the dough into four sections, and roll them out into long strings that are between 1/4 and a 1/2 inch in diameter. Cut the strings into 1-inch pieces, and lay them on parchment paper until you're ready to cook them.

3. Bring the salted water to a boil, and add the gnudi with a slotted spoon or wire basket. Return the water to a boil, reduce the heat to a simmer. Cook, occasionally stirring, for about 8 minutes or until there is no gumminess when you taste one. Drain.

4. Toss with the remaining Parmesan and the butter, and serve immediately.

1 twelve-ounce package frozen winter
squash, thawed

1 cup ricotta cheese

2 eggs

1/4 cup grated Parmesan cheese plus
2 tablespoons for serving

3 cups flour plus flour for the
work surface

1/2 teaspoon ground nutmeg

1/2 teaspoon dried sage

1/2 teaspoon salt plus 3 tablespoons
for the cooking water

1/4 teaspoon freshly ground pepper

6 quarts water for cooking

3 tablespoons butter

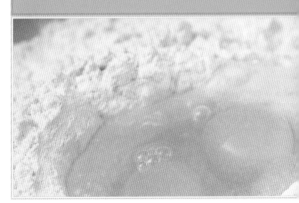

Cornish Pastry

Cornish Pasties

Aren't these pies? Well . . . if they're pies, they're dumpling-shaped pies—or maybe pies doing a dumpling's job. Still, they're wrapped in dough and have filling inside, and therefore you'll find recipes for them right here. Pasties also epitomize an important subset of the dumpling universe: the portable meal. They can be made ahead, taken anywhere, and eaten hot, warm, or cold.

In England, Cornish pasties have become a sort of national snack food: something a bit more homegrown than burgers or pizza but still with a touch of the exotic because they come from Cornwall—about as far away from big cities as you can get and still be in the same country.

Yes, there is what you might call a "proper" pasty. It uses a pie crust along with a filling of beef and root vegetables, but that's only the start; vegetarian, pork, and curry are all common pasties these days, and one even sees fish. Remember, though, that people whose main interest is in upholding the ancient traditions of Cornwall will recoil at the thought of anything from the sea in their pasty and politely decline almost anything other than beef and root vegetables.

Proper Wrappers for Cornish Pasties

Makes 6 wrappers

This is the part that makes you think a pasty is a pie; the dough is mainly flour and fat with just a bit of salt. But it's not supposed to be flaky—if it were, it the whole thing would crumble when you picked it up.

3 cups all-purpose flour

1/2 cup shortening (see note)

1/2 cup margarine

1 teaspoon salt

NOTE: Substitute lard if you can get something better than the stuff in the supermarket. See page 269 for more details.

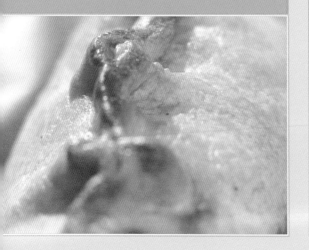

1. Put the flour, shortening, margarine, and salt in a large bowl. Mix them together by pinching the flour into the fat until it's all been saturated. If a dough hasn't formed by the time every last lump of fat has been broken up, add water 1 tablespoon at a time until it does. Wrap the dough in plastic wrap, and refrigerate for at least 30 minutes. If need be, it can stay refrigerated all day.

2. Slice the dough into 8 equal parts, and form each into a ball. On a floured work surface, roll out the ball into a flat disk about 4 or 5 inches in diameter (use a large cookie cutter or a small bowl as a template). The wrappers are now ready to be filled and baked. If you're not going to fill the wrappers immediately, cover them with parchment or wax paper and refrigerate; they'll keep for at least a day or two.

Variation:Whole-Grain Wrappers for Pasties
In the U.K., vegetarians and health-food enthusiasts are a very visible part of food culture, and a pasty with a whole-grain wrapper and vegetarian filling (see page 223) wouldn't be an unusual offering.

To make whole-grain wrapper dough, follow the instructions for "Proper Wrappers for Cornish Pasties," but instead of using 3 cups of unbleached all-purpose flour, use 1 cup of unbleached all-purpose flour and 2 cups of whole-wheat flour. It's possible to make a crust that's 100 percent whole wheat, but it might be a bit too crumbly.

Filling, Forming, and Cooking Cornish Pasties

Cornish legend tells of boiled pasties and even tiny ones served in broth, but in reality, the proper way to cook them is baking. Even in legend there's only one way to form a pasty: a variation on the half-moon fold, with the seam across the top. Let's go over the details.

Vegetable oil or vegetable oil spray

1. Preheat your oven to 325 degrees.

2. Spoon 2 tablespoons of filling into the center of a dough disk. Grasp two opposite corners of the disk, and bring them together on top of the filling. Pinch them shut. Now pinch the whole thing closed with the seam running across the top. (See step-by-step photos.)

3. Place the sealed pasties on a well-oiled cookie sheet, and bake for 1 hour and 15 minutes or until the crust is golden and the meat and root vegetables are fully cooked and tender.

4. Serve warm with a bit of brown sauce or ketchup. Pasties are really portable and the perfect thing to bring when you're brown-bagging it and don't feel like a sandwich.

Traditional Beef and Turnip Pasty

Makes 6 pasties

It's almost compulsory to start our pasty recipes here—and for good reason: This is the "proper" pasty and the one by which all others are judged. We have other fillings, and even more can be found in snack shops all over England, but beef and those root vegetables are where the whole thing began.

FILLING

1 cup finely chopped onion
    (about 1 medium onion)

1 cup finely chopped potato (about
    1 small or medium potato)

1 cup finely chopped turnip (about
    1 turnip)

1cup finely chopped chuck steak
    (not ground; about 8 ounces)

1 tablespoon Worcestershire sauce

1/2 teaspoon salt

1/4 teaspoon freshly ground black pepper

WRAPPERS

"Proper Wrappers for Cornish Pasties,"
    page 218, or "Whole-Grain Pastry
    Wrappers for Pasties," page 218

1. To make the filling, combine the onion, potato, turnip, steak, Worcestershire sauce, salt, and pepper in a large bowl, and mix until all the ingredients are well distributed. If you're not going to fill the wrappers immediately, refrigerate the mixture until ready.

2. To make the dumplings, see "Filling, Forming, and Cooking Cornish Pasties," page 219.

Local Pubs: Something British on the Menu

If you tried to guess which foreign country's cuisine was most popular in the U.S.A. based on the fame of cookbook authors and television hosts, Great Britain would win by a mile. Jamie Oliver, Gordon Ramsay, and a bunch of others give the impression that Americans are devouring the food of the United Kingdom at every chance. Sadly, nothing can be further from the truth. In the New York area, home to a huge number of British expats, there are only a handful of places where a person can find a Sunday roast, smoked kippers, or a Cornish pasty.

The Ship Inn in Milford, New Jersey, is a typical example of this very untypical genre. Here, Chef Lonnie Lippert presides over a kitchen that would be respectable in the Cotswolds, a London suburb, or a resort/fishing village in Cornwall. When it was time to talk pasties, though, he turned me over to his trusty British assistant, Hertfordshire native James Griffiths.

James didn't waste a second. While I was still unpacking my laptop, he hauled out two giant dumpling presses made just for pasties plus a huge rolling pin and got right to work. Moments later, the dough was rolled out, the filling was mixed, and perfectly formed pasties were emerging from his presses.

James's pasties were "tiddy oggies," or British navy style, with a ground-meat filling and gravy on top. People I had spoken to in Cornwall about this told me that gravy on a pasty was an abomination—but obviously they never debated the subject with a chef holding a 20-pound rolling pin.

Afterward we sat in the pub's dining room, and I saw that this place was "authentic" in the classic restaurant sense. Great beers (brewed right on the premises) are served with meals that would make or Jamie Oliver beam with satisfaction. Roast beef and Yorkshire pudding, toad in the hole, and bangers and mash are presented in a room whose warm wood and brass make it feel like a better pub in a small, scenic English town. (Painswick? Kettlewell? Padstow?) In fact, when I left the building, the shock of seeing New Jersey—albeit one of the nicest towns in the state—was almost too much to bear.

Vegetarian Onion and Turnip Pasty

Makes 6 pasties

Since a pasty is known for being meat filled, what do those who don't eat meat do when it's time for the rest of us to down a few? Eat some of these.

1. To make the filling, combine the onion, potato, turnip, carrot, celery, salt, andpepper in a large bowl, and mix until all the ingredients are well distributed. If you're not going to fill the wrappers immediately, refrigerate the mixture until ready.

2. So what's that butter for? When you've put your filling on the disk of dough and before you seal your pasty up, put a dab of butter in there. It's traditional and will add a great bit of flavor. And don't forget that butter! Although vegans can use olive oil instead.

3. To make the dumplings, see "Filling, Forming, and Cooking Cornish Pasties," page 219.

FILLING

1 cup finely chopped onion (about 1 medium onion)

1 cup finely chopped potato (about 1 small or medium potato)

1 cup finely chopped turnip (about 1 turnip)

1/2 cup finely chopped carrot (about 1 medium carrot)

1/2 cup finely chopped celery (about 1 celery stalk)

1/2 teaspoon salt

1/4 teaspoon freshly ground black pepper

1/4 cup butter or olive oil

WRAPPERS

"Whole-Grain Pastry Wrappers for Pasties," page 218

Mild Curried Lamb Pasty

Makes 6 pasties

If you're looking for a traditional and "proper" pasty recipe, this one—filled with curried lamb—won't even be close. But if instead you want something popular and even kind of contemporary, this pasty fits the bill. It's the sort of snack you'll find in train stations, fancy bakeries, and even at Cornish surfing resorts.

FILLING

1 cup finely chopped onion
         (about 1 medium onion)

2 tablespoons mild curry paste
         (see note)

1 pound ground lamb

1 teaspoon salt

1/2 teaspoon freshly ground
         black pepper

NOTE: Please use the paste that comes
         in a jar, not a powder.

WRAPPERS

"Proper Wrappers for Cornish Pasties,"
         page 218, or "Whole-Grain
         Pastry Wrappers for Pasties,"
         page 218

1. To make the filling, combine the onion, curry paste, lamb, salt, and pepper in a large bowl and mix really well; your hands are great here. If you're not going to fill the wrappers immediately, refrigerate the mixture until ready.

2. To make the dumplings, see "Filling, Forming, and Cooking Cornish Pasties," page 219.

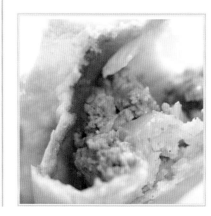

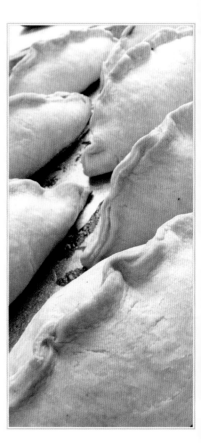

In England, Tea Goes with Everything

The first time you eat in one of those café/snack shops that are all over Great Britain, you'll probably have one of their incredible "puddings"—a sweet dessert with gobs of whipped cream and, of course, a pot of tea on the side. If you go a bit deeper into the local food scene, you'll have fish and chips in a restaurant: deep-fried fish fillets, fried potatoes that they insist on calling "chips," and a small cup of "mushy peas" (not mushy and not exactly peas, but I didn't name them). And to wash it down? Tea. Foreign tourists and young, sophisticated types might go for beer or soda, but tea is the drink of choice, not to mention tradition. So it should come as no surprise that when you're out in the farthest reaches of Cornwall, and your food of choice is a pasty, more often than not you'll be offered tea along with it.

For reasons I can't begin to speculate over, English tea has unique powers of refreshment. Make it with loose leaves and a tiny strainer or even with a good imported tea bag, sweeten it with a spoonful of sugar, lighten it up a bit with milk or cream, and there you have it: soda without the fizz, coffee without the acid, and hot cocoa with a lot less sugar. It's very modest, very English, a sort of miracle drink.

THE AMERICAS

Fried Pastel

Brazilian Deep-Fried Pastries (Pastels)

On a hot July day, I set out to find some pastels, those big Brazilian fried dumplings. My criteria for the perfect pastel shop weren't all that demanding: It had to at least have some people eating in it so that it didn't have that empty and depressing feeling, and it needed at least one seat available so that I wouldn't have to wait on line in the sticky summer heat. This wasn't as easy as it sounds!

After wandering the streets of the Ironbound District of Newark, New Jersey, for a half hour, I was finally seated in the right kind of place: The TV was tuned to the Brazilian equivalent of the Weather Channel (it was hotter and damper in New Jersey), the crowd was speaking Portuguese, and there were baskets full of pastels and esfirras (see page 228) on almost every table.

Soon I had some pastels in front of me. They looked like giant, deep-fried empanadas (see page 239). Holding one in my hand, I asked the server, "Is a pastel just a big, fried empanada?" She thought long and hard and then answered, "Yes!" After eating a few, the differences became clearer: crunch from frying, size, and at least a few unique fillings.

It was a classic dumpling find delicious and transforming. The crunch of frying made the day.

Pastel Wrappers

Makes dough for 12 pastels

1. Sift the flour, salt, and baking powder together in a large bowl. Add the margarine, egg, and water, and mix until all the ingredients are well combined. Form the mixture into a dough (your hands work well here). If the dough is dry and cracking, add more water 1 tablespoon at a time until it's moist and springy; if the dough is sticky, add more flour 1 tablespoon at a time until it's smooth. Little bits of flour or water can change things quite a bit at this stage of the game! On a well-floured work surface, knead the dough for 5 to 7 minutes—a poke with a finger will cause it to bounce back like a soft pillow. Cover the dough with plastic wrap, and refrigerate for 30 minutes.

3 cups all-purpose flour plus flour for work surface

1 teaspoon salt

1/2 teaspoon baking powder

2 tablespoons margarine, at room temperature

1 egg

1 cup water

Filling, Forming, and Cooking Pastels

Here, we're using the same folding method as "Cajun Meat Pies" (page 264) and "Dried Fruit Fried Pies" (page 266), only pastels are a bit bigger.

3 quarts peanut oil for frying

1. Slice off a piece from the ball of wrapper dough, and form it into a ball the size of a Ping-Pong ball. On a floured work surface, roll out the ball into a flat sheet, and cut out a 6-inch diameter disk (use a large cookie cutter or a small bowl as a template). Make the next wrapper by combining the scraps from the previous one with some more sliced from the "mother" block.

2. Spoon 2 tablespoons of the filling into the center of the dough disk. Fold the disk over using the traditional "Half-Moon Fold" (see page 25), and then use a fork to seal the edges.

3. Heat the oil in a heavy pot over medium or medium-high heat and stir occasionally until the oil reaches 375 degrees. Gently lower the pastels into the oil using a slotted spoon or wire basket made for this purpose. Continue cooking for about 5 minutes or until the dumplings are golden brown. Remove them from the oil using the same utensil you used to put them in. Drain on paper towels before serving.

4. Serve warm with hot sauce on the side.

Hearts of Palm Pastels

Makes 12 pastels

Here's one of those truly rare South American vegetarian fillings.

1. To make the filling, heat the oil in a skillet over medium heat. Add the potato, onion, garlic, and pepper, and cook and stir for about 20 minutes or until the edges of the onions turn brown and the potatoes are fork tender. Mix in the hearts of palm, parsley, salt, and pepper, and continue cooking and stirring for about 10 minutes or until the hearts are warmed through and all the ingredients are evenly distributed. When the filling mixture is done, remove from the heat, set it aside, and let cool.

2. To make the dumplings, see "Filling, Forming, and Cooking Pastels," page 230.

FILLING

2 tablespoons olive oil

1 cup peeled, chopped white potato (about 1 medium; Russets work fine)

1 cup chopped onion (about 1 medium onion)

3 garlic cloves, minced

1/2 cup chopped green bell pepper (about 1 small bell pepper)

1 cup drained, chopped canned hearts of palm

1/4 cup chopped fresh Italian parsley

1 teaspoon salt

1/2 teaspoon freshly ground black pepper

WRAPPERS

"Pastel Wrappers," page 229

Shrimp Pastels

Makes 12 pastels

People always seem to be surprised by the creamy sauce in these. They're nothing at all like "Cantonese Shrimp Dumplings" (see page 51).

FILLING

1 tablespoon margarine

2 tablespoons all-purpose flour

1 cup milk

2 tablespoons peanut oil

1 cup chopped onion
    (about 1 medium onion)

1 cup chopped fresh tomato
    (about 1 medium tomato)

2 cups chopped raw shrimp
    (about 8 ounces)

1/2 teaspoon salt

WRAPPERS

"Pastel Wrappers," page 229

1. To make the filling, melt the margarine in a small saucepan over medium heat. Add the flour, stirring continuously and making sure that no lumps form. Slowly add the milk; a thick sauce should form immediately. Remove from the heat, and set aside.

2. Heat the oil in a skillet over medium heat. Add the onion, and cook and stir for about 5 minutes or until the onions become translucent. Add the tomato, and continue cooking for about 20 more minutes or until most of the resulting liquid evaporates. Mix in the shrimp and salt, and continue cooking for another 2 minutes or until the shrimp is opaque white.

3. Pour the milk sauce over the cooked shrimp, and mix well. When the filling mixture is done, remove from the heat, set it aside, and let cool.

4. To make the dumplings, see "Filling, Forming, and Cooking Pastels," page 230.

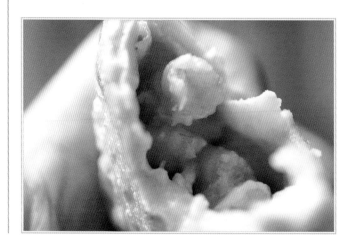

Brazilian "Arab-Style" Little Pies (Esfirras)

I thought I had esfirras figured out. To me, they didn't look all that different than the little snacks served in bars all over Portugal—the link was obvious. But when I sat down to taste my first esfirra, the menu of my local Brazilian snack shop called it "Arabian Pastry" (which I would more accurately deem "Arab-Style"). I guess it wasn't so obvious after all.

A bit more digging and I learned that there's a huge Middle Eastern population in Brazil. Once alerted, I began to notice that restaurants that catered to the local Brazilian community served kebabs, kibbe, and even something called a "cigarette"—the local version of the Turkish cigar.

Esfirra Wrappers

Makes dough for 10 esfirras

Even though these are often called Arab-Style or Arabian pastries on English menus, don't substitute the Middle Eastern "Yeast Pie Wrappers" (page 120). Despite that translation of its name, the recipe is as Brazilian as it gets; it even uses margarine.

1 cup water (see note)

1 packet active dry yeast

3 cups all-purpose flour plus flour
    for work surface

1 teaspoon sugar

1 teaspoon salt

2 tablespoons margarine,
    at room temperature

1 egg

NOTE: I find that I get much better results using bottled water, because the chlorine in my tap water kills the yeast before it can rise.

1. Warm the water to 90 degrees, and sprinkle the yeast on the surface. Let it stand for 10 minutes or until it begins to bubble a bit. This confirms that the yeast is alive and ready to work.

2. Sift the flour, sugar, and salt together in a large bowl. Then add the margarine and egg and mix with your hands until a dough starts to form. If the dough is dry and cracking, add water 1 tablespoon at a time until it's moist and springy; if the dough is sticky, add flour 1 tablespoon at a time until it's smooth. On a floured work surface, knead the dough for about 5 minutes or until a poke with a finger causes it to bounce back like a soft pillow.

3. Divide the prepared dough into 10 equal pieces. Roll each piece into a small ball, and store them where they won't be disturbed for 3 hours. At the time they'll have doubled in size.

4. To make the dumplings, see "Filling, Forming, and Cooking Esfirras," page 235.

Filling, Forming, and Cooking Esfirras

1. Preheat your oven to 375 degrees.

2. Roll out one section of the raised dough into a flat square. It need not be anywhere near perfect; this is a very forgiving fold.

3. Spoon 2 tablespoons of filling into the center of the dough square. Then lift the corners of the dough, one at a time, and bring them over to the center (see photos).

4. Place the finished pies on a well-oiled cookie sheet, and brush with egg wash. Bake for about 45 minutes or until the crust is golden brown. Serve warm with hot sauce.

Vegetable oil or vegetable oil spray

1 lightly beaten egg for egg wash

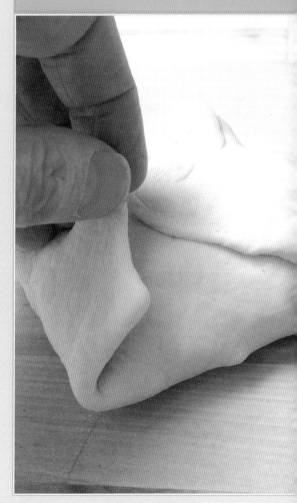

1.

2.

3.

4.

Ground-Beef Esfirras

Makes 10 esfirras

Yes, these little pockets look Arabic, but this filling tells a slightly different story.

FILLING

1 tablespoon peanut oil

1 cup chopped onion
(about 1 medium onion)

1 cup chopped fresh tomato
(about 1 medium tomato)

1 cup chopped red bell pepper
(about 1 pepper)

1 pound ground beef

1 teaspoon salt

1/2 teaspoon freshly ground
black pepper

WRAPPERS

"Esfirra Wrappers," page 234

1. To make the filling, heat the oil in a skillet over medium heat. Add the onion, and cook and stir for about 5 minutes or until the onion has turned translucent and the edges begin to brown. Add the tomato and pepper, and continue cooking for about 5 more minutes or until the pepper is limp. Mix in the beef, salt, and pepper, and cook for about 20 minutes or until the meat is well browned and crumbly. Use the back of a wooden spoon to break up any lumps. Remove the filling mixture from the heat, set it aside, and let cool.

2. To make the dumplings, see "Filling, Forming, and Cooking Esfirras," page 235.

Cheese Esfirras

Makes 10 esfirras

OK, you may not be lucky enough to find Brazilian Catupiry™ cheese, but the combination of Muenster, cream cheese, and ricotta does a great job in its place. (Tip: If you do find it, use 1 1/2 cups of Catupiry™ instead of the Muenster and cream cheese.)

1. To make the filling, melt the Muenster in a double boiler on very low heat. Add the cream cheese, ricotta, salt, and pepper. After about 3 minutes, the cheeses will be soft enough to blend together. Mix until they're well combined, transfer to a coverable plastic container, and refrigerate.

2. To make the dumplings, see "Filling, Forming, and Cooking Esfirras," page 235.

FILLING

1/2 cup chopped Muenster cheese
    (about 2 ounces)

1 cup cream cheese

1 1/2 cups ricotta cheese

1/2 teaspoon salt

1/2 teaspoon freshly ground white pepper

WRAPPERS

"Esfirra Wrappers," page 234

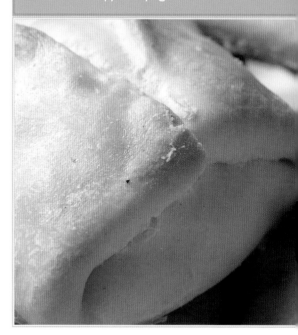

Baked Empanada

Latin American Baked Pastries: Empanadas

There are places that people always associate with empanadas: those bakeries where everybody reads the newspapers in Spanish, and the smell of good, strong coffee is in the air; the snack trucks that stand on the sidelines of local soccer-league playoffs; and restaurants that represent almost every country in South America, where they can be found as a breakfast item, on a lunch platter, or a dinner appetizer.

We Americans tend to think that empanadas come from Latin America, but they originated in the Galicia region of Spain. The name is rooted in the Spanish verb *empanar,* meaning "to bread," "to coat with bread," or "to wrap in bread." And that's just what they are: a bit of something—almost always strongly seasoned—with a bit of dough surrounding it.

Empanada Wrappers

Makes dough for 10 empanadas

In the New World, even the dough has New World ingredients.

2 cups all-purpose flour

1 cup finely ground cornmeal (sometimes called "corn flour")

1/2 cup shortening

1/2 teaspoon salt

1/2 teaspoon baking powder

1. Mix the flour, cornmeal, shortening, salt, and baking powder in a bowl. Use your fingers to pinch the dry ingredients into the shortening until they begin to combine. Then add water 1 tablespoon at a time, and knead the mixture until a dough forms. Knead for an additional 2 minutes. Form the dough into a ball, wrap it in plastic, and refrigerate for at least 30 minutes.

2. To make the dumplings, see "Forming, Filling, and Cooking Empanadas," page 241.

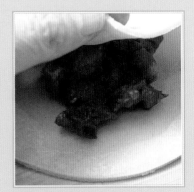

Filling, Forming, and Cooking Empanadas

1. Preheat your oven to 375 degrees.

2. Slice the empanada dough into 10 pieces. Form each piece into a smaller ball. On a floured work surface, roll them out into flat disks about 4 inches in diameter (use a cookie cutter or small bowl as a template). The wrappers are now ready to be filled and cooked.

3. Spoon 1 1/2 tablespoons of filling into the center of the disk, fold it in half, and pinch the edges into a wide, flat, margin. Fold the flat area back toward the empanada to create a ridge along the seam. Then use a fork to seal and crimp the edges. Check out the accompanying photos to see how this works.

4. Oil a cookie sheet, and lay out the formed empanadas, leaving a bit of space between them. Use a brush to coat the top of each one with beaten egg. Bake for about 45 minutes or until the crust is golden. Serve warm with a good hot sauce or salsa. (See "Salsa Cruda," page 247, for a recipe suggestion.)

Vegetable oil or vegetable oil spray

1 lightly beaten egg for egg wash

Beef and Raisin Empanadas

Makes 10 empanadas

This is the *World of Dumplings* version of picadillo, the seasoned ground-meat mixture found all over Latin America. As an empanada filling, it's a good, basic start.

FILLING

1 tablespoon olive oil

1 teaspoon ground cumin

1/4 teaspoon ground cinnamon

2 whole cloves

1 cup chopped onion
        (about 1 medium onion)

4 cloves garlic, chopped

2 jalapeño peppers, chopped
        (remove the seeds to make
        the dish milder)

1 pound ground beef

1/2 teaspoon salt

1/4 teaspoon freshly ground
        black pepper

1 cup chopped fresh tomato
        (about 1 medium tomato)

1/2 cup raisins

1/2 chopped pitted olives

WRAPPERS

"Empanada Wrappers," page 240

1. To make the filling, heat the olive oil in a skillet over medium heat. Add the cumin, cinnamon, cloves, onion, garlic, and peppers, and cook and stir for about 5 minutes or until the onions become translucent. Then add the beef, salt, and pepper. Continue cooking, stirring occasionally, until the meat is well browned. Add the tomato and raisins. The filling is done when the raisins are softened. Remove the mixture from the heat, set it aside, and let cool. If you're not going to fill the wrappers immediately, refrigerate the mixture until ready.

2. To make the dumplings, see "Filling, Forming, and Cooking Empanadas," page 241.

Chicken Empanadas

Makes 10 empanadas

This filling is a version of the classic mole stew that is found all over Mexico. And, yes, it's that legendary "chicken with chocolate sauce." (By the way, this is another one of those recipes using no salt or pepper; the various ingredients add enough of both not to require any additional.)

1. To make the filling, heat the olive oil in a skillet over medium heat. Add the cumin, cinnamon, chipotle peppers with sauce, onion, and garlic, and cook and stir for about 5 minutes or until the onions become translucent. Add the chicken, and continue cooking, stirring occasionally, for about 10 minutes or until the chicken is thoroughly cooked. Mix in the tomatoes and chocolate and stir continually—don't slack off on the stirring here or it will scorch—and cook for about 5 more minutes or until all the ingredients have fully combined. When the filling mixture is done, remove from the heat, set it aside, and let cool. If you're not going to fill the wrappers immediately, refrigerate the mixture until ready.

2. To make the dumplings, see "Filling, Forming, and Cooking Empanadas," page 241.

FILLING

1 tablespoon olive oil

1/2 teaspoon ground cumin

1/4 teaspoon ground cinnamon

2 chipotle peppers in adobo, finely chopped, plus 1 teaspoon sauce from the can

1/2 cup chopped onion (about 1 small onion)

3 cloves garlic, chopped

2 cups finely chopped boneless chicken (about 1 pound; see note)

1 cup canned crushed tomatoes

1/2 square unsweetened baking chocolate (1/2 ounce)

NOTE: It's much easier to chop the chicken if you put it in the freezer for a few minutes first.

WRAPPERS

"Empanada Wrappers," page 240

Spinach Empanadas

Makes 10 empanadas

I hope you didn't come to this page looking for something vegetarian. This Latin American recipe has spinach, but it also has bacon, boiled eggs, and cheese. It's a great treat, but it's more of a way to get bacon fans to eat their spinach. In fact, it's a fabulous way to encourage vegetable eating. (And don't be tempted to add salt; the bacon provides plenty.)

FILLING

1/2 cup chopped bacon

1/2 cup chopped onion
(about 1 small onion)

1 package (10 ounces) frozen chopped
spinach

1 egg, hard-cooked, chopped

1/2 cup Mexican white cheese
(queso blanco), crumbled

1/2 teaspoon freshly ground
black pepper

1/4 teaspoon ground nutmeg

WRAPPERS

"Empanada Wrappers," page 240

1. To make the filling, heat the bacon in a skillet over medium-high heat. Cook and stir for about 4 minutes or until the bacon starts to turn golden. Lower the heat to medium, add the onion, and continue cooking and stirring for about 5 more minutes or until the onion becomes transparent. Mix in the spinach, egg, cheese, pepper, and nutmeg, making sure that all the ingredients are well combined. When the filling mixture is done, remove from the heat, set it aside, and let cool. If you're not going to fill the wrappers immediately, refrigerate the mixture until ready.

2. To make the dumplings, see "Filling, Forming, and Cooking Empanadas," page 241.

Sweet Potato Empanadas

Makes 15 empanadas

I'm not really sure why I thought sweet potatoes were a cold-climate/cold-weather ingredient, but here it is: a tropical dessert made from what is often thought of as a wintry side dish.

1. To make the filling, mix the potato, butter, sugar, molasses, almonds, milk, nutmeg, and cinnamon in a large bowl, making sure that all the ingredients are well blended. If you're not going to fill the wrappers immediately, refrigerate the mixture until ready.

2. To make the dumplings, see "Filling, Forming, and Cooking Empanadas," page 241.

FILLING

3 cups cooked, mashed sweet potatoes (about 5 medium potatoes)

2 tablespoons butter, softened

1/4 cup brown sugar

1/4 cup molasses

1/4 cup crushed almonds

1/4 cup sweetened condensed milk

1/2 teaspoon ground nutmeg

1/2 teaspoon ground cinnamon

WRAPPERS

"Empanada Wrappers," page 240

Corn and Black Bean Empanadas

Makes 10 empanadas

How's this for a New World empanada?
A filling whose main ingredients are classics
of the place: corn and black beans.

FILLING

1 cup canned black beans,
     rinsed and drained

1 cup corn kernels
     (frozen are fine here)

1/2 cup Mexican white cheese
     (queso blanco), crumbled

1/4 cup chopped scallions

2 chipotle peppers, finely chopped
     (add more for additional heat)

1/2 teaspoon ground cumin

1/2 teaspoon salt

1/2 teaspoon freshly ground
     black pepper

WRAPPERS

"Empanada Wrappers," page 240

1. To make the filling, put the beans in a large bowl, and mash them until none are whole and a paste begins to form. Add the corn, cheese, scallions, chipotles, cumin, salt, and pepper, and mix until all the ingredients are well distributed. If you're not going to fill the wrappers immediately, refrigerate the mixture until ready.

2. To make the dumplings, see "Filling, Forming, and Cooking Empanadas," page 241.

Side Dish: Spicy Raw Vegetable Sauce (Salsa Cruda)

Makes 2 cups

Like simple tomato sauce, salsa cruda, or "raw sauce," is easy to make at home and available in endless forms at almost every food store in the country. Like tomato sauce, though, simple salsas lose something in the bottling; after all, once it's packed, it's not even raw anymore. A fresh, homemade salsa is almost always worthwhile. Give this one a try.

In a large nonmetallic bowl, combine the tomato, tomatillo, jalapeño, onion, garlic, cilantro, salt, pepper, and lime juice. Mix well, cover, and refrigerate for at least 4 hours or until the flavors have completely combined. Store covered in the refrigerator.

1 cup chopped fresh tomato
(about 1 large tomato)

1/4 cup chopped fresh tomatillo
(about 2 tomatillos)

1 fresh jalapeño pepper, finely chopped

1/2 cup chopped red onion
(about 1 medium onion)

2 cloves garlic, finely chopped

1/4 cup finely chopped fresh
cilantro leaves

1/2 teaspoon salt

1/4 teaspoon freshly ground black pepper

1 tablespoon lime juice

Your Local Latin American Grocery: A Shopping Guide

When I head over to my favorite Latin American grocery, I announce that I'm going to the "Supremo." For some reason, it never occurred to anybody that this was the actual name of the place rather than my description of it. So when I'd bring them there for the first time, there'd always be exclamations like, "It really *is* the Supremo!"

Nowadays your local Latin American grocery might not be a tiny corner shop with cans of beans and cellophane bags of dried herbs. It's just as likely to be huge and feature full-service meat, fish, produce, and bakery sections. Large Hispanic neighborhoods will have even more depth, with specialty stores that offer vividly flavored artisanal products.

Here are some things to look for:

Beans: Even though they're dried or canned, freshness is the key word. In most supermarkets the dried-bean selection is limited to a few lonely plastic bags. Here, there's more variety and turnover, so you'll get a fresher product. Freshness might not sound like something that applies here, but if you've ever had beans that didn't become tender no matter how long you cooked them, they almost certainly were stale. Canned beans are pretty much the same story here: There are more different kinds, they sell faster, and, more often than not, prices are far lower.

Cheese: When you think about supermarket cheese, what often comes to mind are wedges of brown

and yellow stuff from Europe. But here the cheeses—with names like *queso blanco, queso de freir, queso Boricuca, queso fresco,* and *queso Colombiano*—are all white. They're all meant for cooking, and each has properties that chefs from their home country crave. Queso blanco is a perfect example: Heat it up and it softens, but heat it more, and it still doesn't melt. This means that it gives foods an entirely different texture than a traditional American choice like Monterey Jack (which melts quickly and is absorbed into the rest of the dish, sometimes with little trace of itself).

Meat: I doubt that "meat-o-centric" is a word, but it certainly describes many Latin American cuisines. The great steaks of Argentina, the moles of Mexico (see page 241 for some stuffed into an empanada), and the grilled dishes of Colombia are all meat based, and shoppers expect something more than steaks and hamburger. Tripe, hooves, and salted fatback are all available at the Supremo. Chorizo, a single item in most stores, is a whole section there.

Produce: I expected papaya, mango, and jicama. I hoped for batata, nopal, and chayote. It turns out that all were there, and much more: Savia cactus and all sorts of large, brown, potatolike roots that could well be the subject of an entire book.

Spices: All those dried chilies are bound to catch your eye; *cascabel,* California, *ancho, guajillo, negro, arbol, puya,* and *pasilla* were all on display during my last visit. Each of these has a different flavor and aroma, and the selection gives you a fighting chance at authentic flavors.

249

Jamaican Patty Wrappers

Jamaican Patties

Ask the average person what the spiciest cuisine is, and the answer will almost always be Thai or Mexican. But my vote goes for Jamaican; their Scotch bonnet peppers are the hottest, and cooks there aren't the least bit bashful about using them.

The next question is: "Are Jamaican patties really even cuisine?" Many seem to think of them as being in the same category as chicken nuggets; that is, a food that didn't exist before modern industrial processing. But Jamaican patties, no matter how we think of them today, are part of a vibrant culinary heritage. And they taste really good, too—especially if you like things really spicy.

Jamaican Patty Wrappers
Makes enough dough for 12 patties

In Jamaica, even the dough is spicy . . . .

1. Sift the flour, curry powder , and salt together in a large bowl, and make sure they're well combined. Add the margarine and shortening, and pinch the flour and fat together until they are completely mixed and coarse grains have formed. Add the water, and mix until a dough forms. If the dough is dry and cracking, add water 1 tablespoon at a time until it's moist and springy; if the dough is sticky, add more flour 1 tablespoon at a time until it's smooth.

2. On a floured work surface, knead the dough for 5 to 7 minutes or until a poke with a finger causes it to bounce back like a soft pillow. Wrap the dough in plastic wrap, and refrigerate for at least 30 minutes before using.

3 cups all-purpose flour, plus flour for the work surface

2 tablespoons Jamaican curry powder

1/2 teaspoon salt

1/2 cup margarine (1 stick)

1/2 cup shortening

1/2 cup cold water

Filling, Forming, and Cooking Jamaican Patties

Vegetable oil or vegetable oil spray

1. Preheat your oven to 425 degrees.

2. Slice off a 1 1/2-inch piece from the ball of wrapper dough. Roll it out into a flat sheet, and cut out a 6-inch-diameter disk (use a large cookie cutter or small bowl as a template). Make the next wrapper by combining the scraps from the previous one with some more sliced from the "mother" block.

3. Spoon 2 tablespoons of filling into the center of the dough disk. Fold the disk over using the traditional "Half-Moon Fold" (see page 25), and then use a fork to seal the edges. Place the sealed patties on a well-oiled cookie sheet, and bake for 30 minutes or until the crust is firm and beginning to brown. Serve immediately.

Variations:

In Jamaican restaurants, patties are sometimes served as a sandwich filling with coco bread on the outside. And believe it or not, you can also find people who put hot sauce on them.

Jamaican Beef Patties

Makes 12 patties

Note that even this relatively mild recipe has scorching hot Scotch bonnet peppers. This is *not* for the meek.

1. To make the filling, heat the oil in a skillet over medium heat. Add the salt, pepper, curry powder, and thyme, and stir until all the ingredients are coated with oil and no dry powder remains in the pan. Mix in the onion and Scotch bonnet pepper, and cook and stir for about 5 minutes or until the onion is transparent and the pepper is limp. Add the beef, and cook it with vigorous stirring for about 10 minutes or until it's browned and crumbled. There should be no lumps of either spices or ground beef. When the filling mixture is done, remove from the heat, set it aside, and let cool.

2. To make the dumplings, see "Filling, Forming, and Cooking Jamaican Patties," page 252.

FILLING

1 tablespoon peanut oil

1 teaspoon salt

1/2 teaspoon freshly ground black pepper

1 teaspoon Jamaican curry powder

1 teaspoon dried thyme

1 cup chopped onion
       (about 1 medium onion)

1/2 fresh Scotch bonnet pepper, finely
       chopped (see note)

1 pound ground beef

NOTE: Caution—don't chop with bare hands; these peppers are really, really hot.

WRAPPERS

"Jamaican Patty Wrappers," page 251

Just How Many Patties Can You Eat?

It was rough; security was tight. People were lining up 20 deep and being checked carefully; bags inspected, tickets examined, and credentials challenged at every turn. I tried telling the men in charge that I was on the guest list . . . a V.I.P . . . that I was a Jamaican Patty expert . . . that I belonged inside. . . . "Inside" was the Caribbean Food Delights National Jamaican Patty Eating Competition, itself part of a larger Island festival with food, health exhibits, blasting music, and even a beauty contest in the evening. It was also a perfect place to learn about real Jamaican home cooking—home cooks and picnics were everywhere. As I watched trays of jerk chicken, fried fish, and rice and peas being carried in, I thought that speed eating was the wrong take; they needed to name the best Jamaican home cook.

Arnie "Chowhound" Chapman, the competition's organizer, and Carribean Food Delights, the sponsor, soon got me past the velvet rope and onto the grounds. There, the crew and the real stars—the competitive eaters—were beginning to gather. Fat, thin, men and women, they stood in bunches and sipped water until it was almost show time.

The competition had two categories: amateur and professional. The amateurs were a mix of big eaters and people who were trying to qualify as pro (which required them to have won a certain amount in prize money). It was easy to tell the difference; the newcomers were all big and . . . well . . . *really* big. The professionals? Far fitter and wearing silly hats, fake bowties, or other touches of showmanship.

254

Indeed, moments before they went on stage, the pros were stretching like athletes.

I asked a couple of them what their thoughts were, and they spoke in depth about structure—how patties had a dry crust and a spicy filling. "Gentleman" Joe Menchetti, the pregame favorite, felt that as a past record holder in jalapeño eating, he'd have an advantage from the spiciness. Others spoke of the importance of hydration, pacing, and discipline. All made it clear that even though there was a big joking aspect (the nicknames, the costume items, and the like), they were really serious about how they ate.

These were the ground rules: Each competitor had a platter of patties and a bottle of water in front of them. Standing behind was a person whose job it was to count. The eater who ate the most patties in five minutes was the winner.

Arnie, a woman named Sabrina (her business card read CEO CARIBBEAN FOOD DELIGHTS), and a couple of teenagers dressed in patty costumes took the stage. Arnie then introduced the eaters as if each one were a major sports star, and the crowd went wild. Seconds later they were eating, and I was trying to point my camera between the flying bits of patty filling and splashes of water.

At the end of the five minutes, Gentleman Joe won the pros by eating 11 patties, and a local guy who had never competed before took the amateurs with 8. Afterward, somebody handed me a can of beer and a single patty; it was enough to fill me up.

Jamaican Spicy Fish Patties

Makes 12 patties

Even though Jamaica is an island surrounded by sea, these patties use tilapia, an easily farmed freshwater fish.

FILLING

1 tablespoon butter

1/2 teaspoon ground turmeric

1 teaspoon dried thyme

1/2 teaspoon ground cumin

1/2 teaspoon ground cardamom

1/4 teaspoon ground ginger

3 cloves garlic, finely chopped

1/2 fresh Scotch bonnet pepper, seeded
      and finely chopped (see note)

1 cup chopped onion
      (about 1 medium onion)

3 cups chopped tilapia fillet
      (about 1 pound)

2 tablespoons chopped fresh chives

2 tablespoons chopped fresh
      Italian parsley

1 cup chopped fresh tomato
      (about 1 medium tomato)

NOTE: Caution—don't chop with bare hands; these peppers are really, really hot.

WRAPPERS

"Jamaican Patty Wrappers," page 251

1. To make the filling, melt the butter in a skillet over medium-low heat. Mix in the turmeric, thyme, cumin, cardamom, and ginger, gently stirring until all the spices are coated with butter and no dry powder remains in the pan. Add the garlic, pepper, and onion, and continue cooking, stirring occasionally, for about 10 minutes or until the onion has turned translucent and the edges brown. Now add the tilapia, chives, parsley, and tomato, and simmer for about 20 more minutes or until most of the liquid has evaporated and a thick paste remains. When the filling mixture is done, remove from the heat, set it aside, and let cool.

2. To make the dumplings, see "Filling, Forming, and Cooking Jamaican Patties," page 252.

Dried Fruit Fried Pies

North American Pie and Dumpling Wrappers

Makes wrapper dough for 4 to 24 dumplings

This is the "All-American" crust that we use for "Pennsylvania Dutch Apple Dumplings" (see page 262), "Cajun Meat Pies" (see page 264), and "Dried Fruit Fried Pies" (see page 266).

3 cups all-purpose flour

1/2 teaspoon double-acting
      baking powder

1/2 teaspoon salt

1/2 cup lard (see "The Perfect Piecrust
      Contains . . . ," page 269)

1. Sift the flour, baking powder, and salt together in a large bowl, and then add the lard. Combine the lard with the flour by pinching bits of lard and flour together, then working the mixture with your hands until you have what seems like a bowl of little dough pills. Make sure you have no blobs of lard or cakes of flour. Now add cold water 1 tablespoon at a time, and mix it in until a dough forms. If the dough is dry and cracking, add more water 1 tablespoon at a time until it's moist and springy; if the dough is too sticky, add more flour 1 tablespoon at a time until it's smooth. When you have a pliable dough, shape it into a ball, wrap it in plastic, and refrigerate for at least 30 minutes. It can keep for at least a day this way.

2. For apple dumplings, divide the dough into quarters, form each piece into a ball, and roll out each ball into a flat sheet about 8 inches across. Ideally, you'll wind up with a square, but the fold is pretty forgiving. For the smaller pies, cut out disks of dough from these sheets, using a cookie cutter or a small bowl as a template.

Tailgated by Mennonites: In Search of the Apple Dumpling

If you pass through Lancaster County on the Pennsylvania Turnpike, you see what looks like the edge of rural paradise as you zip by. When you exit the highway and start poking around, something different appears: an odd combination of Amish traditions and a tourist world based on shopping and gluttony. Here you'll find buffets as vast as New Jersey shopping malls and supermarkets that offer sugar in 50-pound sacks. Sprawl has taken its toll on Lancaster County, but food specialties like scrapple, shoo-fly pie, and apple dumplings live on.

The day was 6/6/06, and for a superstitious guy like me, it seemed best to spend it in as wholesome a place as possible. I began my search at the Central Market in downtown Lancaster. Like the city itself, the market is gentrifying nicely. Old-line vendors of local meats and farm produce mix with espresso bars and takeout ethnic. ("African" and "German" caught my eye.) The first apple dumpling came from one of those traditional-looking stands with chrome-and-glass display cases and florescent lighting. I bought a shot of espresso to wash it down with and sat at a public table where a group of construction workers just stared at the less-than-common combination.

My dumpling was mild; the only seasoning was a bit of cinnamon. The wrapper was pie crust and the apple peeled and cored. The first sip of my espresso shot erased the apple flavor completely. It was the dessert version of those small-town wontons I found in this very area.

Driving into the countryside, I started scanning the signs at roadside stands, looking for the archetypical apple dumpling. I was driving so slowly that Mennonite ladies with little bonnets were tailgating me. This really *was* apple-dumpling country, though; they're eaten everywhere around here and not even known a hundred miles away.

Although the area's culinary landscape is dominated by mass-feeding operations called "smorgasbords" (no, none serve Swedish dishes of any sort), the torch of traditional food is upheld by a couple of small restaurants that are totally off the beaten path. My next stop was the White Horse Luncheonette in (where else?) White Horse. There, the apple dumpling was an earthy masterpiece of spices, molasses, and intense fruit flavor.

I had hoped to meet the chef, but she turned out to be a camera-shy Amish woman down the road. "The Amish make the best apple dumplings," the blond waitress told me. There was another mystery about the White Horse dumpling; it had no visible seams. Why were they hidden? With a discreet Amish baker in the background, it looked like I'd never find out.

Stupefied with food and buzzing with caffeine, I staggered into my last stop of the day: the Town Hall Restaurant in Blue Ball. Located along with the firehouse right in the town hall building, this place has always been considered a paragon of Lancaster County cooking. As if more proof were needed, apple dumplings were listed as the day's special. The differences were subtle; less spice, more sugar and another sort of crust. (Perhaps with baking powder?) I wanted to join in the lively, local conversation, but instead I focused on finishing my third dumpling in as many hours while locals talked antiques, real estate, food, and politics.

After eating three apple dumplings and drinking five cups of coffee (four American, one espresso) in three hours and twenty minutes—an act of serious gluttony, even by local standards—I was ready to return to my kitchen and get to work.

Apple Dumplings

Most fillings are made from ingredients that are finely chopped, but here we're in for a big switch: a whole peeled and cored apple. It's just one more variation on the big theme—something special on the inside and dough on the outside.

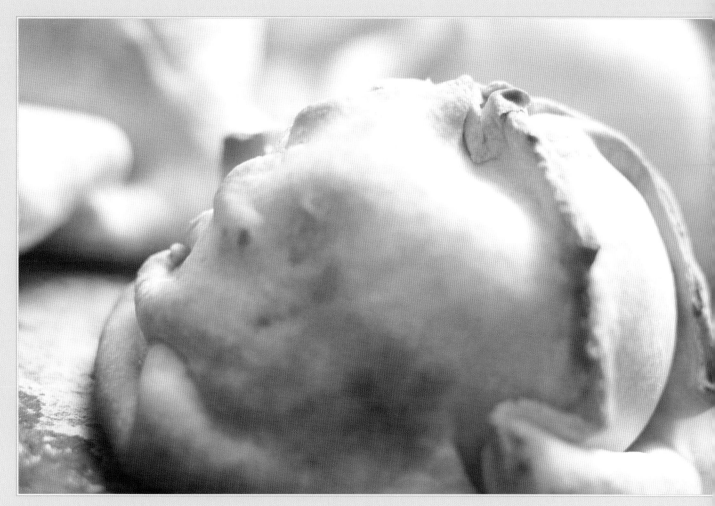

Pennsylvania Dutch Apple Dumplings

Makes 4 dumplings

Legend has it that one Pennsylvania diner made theirs with two apples. We're not going to try anything like that. Instead, we'll aim for the classic: an apple wrapped in dough with a sweet, spicy sauce poured over it. Cream or ice cream can go on top of that, but I don't see the need.

FILLING

1/2 cup brown sugar

1/2 teaspoon ground cinnamon

1/2 teaspoon ground nutmeg

1/4 teaspoon ground cloves

1/2 teaspoon ground ginger

1/2 teaspoon ground cardamom

4 apples, peeled and cored

1/4 cup molasses

WRAPPERS

"North American Pie and Dumpling Wrappers," page 258

Oil for cookie sheet

Sugar sauce (see page 263) for serving

1. Preheat your oven to 375 degrees.

2. To make the filling, combine the brown sugar, cinnamon, nutmeg, cloves, ginger, and cardamom in a small bowl, and mix until well blended.

3. Stand 1 peeled and cored apple in the middle of a wrapper square, spread a tablespoon of molasses on top, and sprinkle one-quarter of the sugar-spice mixture over it. Lift the opposite corners of the dough square, and bring them together. Now pinch the edges to form sealed seams. Place the wrapped apple on a well-oiled cookie sheet, and bake for 1 hour or until the crust is golden brown.

4. Serve with sugar sauce, cream, whipped cream, ice cream, or any combination of the above.

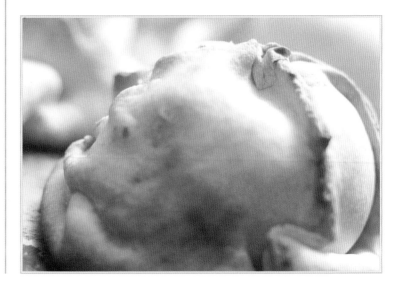

Sugar Sauce for Pennsylvania-Dutch Apple Dumplings

Some people see an apple dumpling as nothing more than a base on which to heap rich things like ice cream, heavy cream, and/or whipped cream. But whatever else you put on, make sure you put some of this on, too.

1. Bring the water to boil in a medium saucepan, and add the molasses, brown sugar, vanilla, cloves, nutmeg, and mace, and stir until all the ingredients are well blended. Reduce the heat to a simmer, and cook for 1 minute with occasional stirring.

2. Serve warm over Pennsylvania Dutch Apple Dumplings (page 262) or almost any fruit pie or even ice cream. It's more versatile than it looks.

1 cup water

1 tablespoon molasses

1/2 cup brown sugar

1 teaspoon vanilla extract

3 whole cloves

1/4 teaspoon ground nutmeg

1/4 teaspoon ground mace

Cajun Meat Pies

Makes 12 pies

"Cajun" is another one of those regional cuisines that I thought I'd find on every local street corner, but instead, there were just high-priced fine-dining restaurants. These little pies—a classic Louisiana snack food—are well worth trying. When you're sitting in some northern city with the snow falling and the wind howling, pop a few of these in the oven, crack open some ice-cold local beer, and feel the heat.

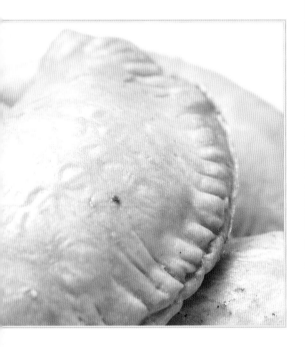

1. To make the filling, heat the oil in a skillet over medium heat. Add the oregano, thyme, paprika, cumin, mace, pepper, and salt, and stir until all the spices are coated with oil and there is no dry powder left. Add the garlic, onion, chili pepper, and scallions. Cook, occasionally stirring, for about 5 minutes or until the onion becomes translucent and the peppers are limp. Mix in the beef and pork, and continue cooking for about 15 minutes or until the meat is

browned and crumbly; you may have to pound the mixture with a wooden spoon a bit. Finally, add the tomatoes, and simmer, occasionally stirring, for about 5 more minutes or until the flavors are well combined. When the filling mixture is done, remove from the heat, set it aside, and let cool.

2. Preheat your oven to 375 degrees.

3. To make the dumplings, slice off about a 1 1/2-inch piece from the big ball of wrapper dough (about the size of Ping-Pong ball). On a floured work surface, roll the ball out into a flat sheet. Cut out a 6-inch-diameter

disk (use a large cookie cutter or small bowl as a template). Make the next wrapper by combining the scraps from the previous one with some more sliced from the "mother" block.

4. Spoon 2 tablespoons of the meat filling into the center of the dough disk. Fold the disk over using the traditional "Half-Moon

Fold" (see page 25), and then use a fork to seal the edges.

5. Lay the folded pies on a well-oiled cookie sheet, and brush the tops with egg wash. Bake for 45 minutes or until the crust is golden brown.

Variation: Deep Frying Cooking Method 3 quarts peanut oil

1. Put the oil in a heavy pot over medium or medium-high heat, and stir occasionally until the oil reaches 375 degrees. Gently lower the dumplings into the oil, using a slotted spoon or wire basket. Cook until the pies are golden brown. Remove from the oil using the same utensil you used to put them in. Drain on paper towels before serving.

2. As a condiment, some people will put out ranch dressing to dampen the heat, though others say that only cold beer will do the trick.

FILLING

1 tablespoon peanut oil

1 teaspoon dried oregano

1 teaspoon dried thyme

1/2 teaspoon paprika

1/2 teaspoon ground cumin

1/2 teaspoon ground mace

1/2 teaspoon freshly ground black pepper

1 teaspoon salt

4 cloves garlic, finely chopped

1 cup chopped onion (about 1 medium onion)

2 tablespoons chopped fresh chili pepper (see note)

2 tablespoons chopped scallions

1/2 pound ground beef

1/2 pound ground pork

1 cup canned diced tomatoes

NOTE: Jalapeños are fine, but don't hesitate to experiment.

WRAPPERS

"North American Pie and Dumpling Wrappers," page 258

Oil spray for cookie sheet

Beaten egg for egg wash

Dried Fruit Fried Pies

Makes 24 pies

For some people, fried pie is something that the big fast-food chains stopped making years ago. Others know it as an American tradition. In Texas and the Deep South, fried pies are cherished classics. And with their filling of dried fruit, a fresh pie can be made any time.

FILLING

2 cups water

1/4 cup brown sugar

1/2 teaspoon ground cinnamon

1/2 teaspoon ground allspice

1/4 teaspoon ground mace

1/4 teaspoon ground cloves

3 cups chopped dried apricots
        (see note)

NOTE: Dried apples or peaches also work well here.

WRAPPERS

"North American Pie and Dumpling Wrappers," page 258

3 quarts peanut oil for frying

1. To make the filling, bring the water to a boil in a medium saucepan, add the brown sugar, cinnamon, allspice, mace, and cloves, and stir until the sugar is dissolved. Lower the heat to a simmer, add the fruit, and continue cooking for about 15 minutes or until the fruit is tender. Drain any excess liquid, and let cool.

2. To make the dumplings, slice off about a 1-inch piece from the ball of wrapper dough. On a floured work surface, roll out the ball into a flat sheet, and cut out a 4 1/2-or 5-inch-diameter disk (use a cookie cutter or small bowl as a template). Make the next wrapper by combining the scraps from the previous one with some more sliced from the "mother" block.

3. Spoon 2 tablespoons of the dried fruit filling into the center of the dough disk. Fold the disk over using the traditional "Half-Moon Fold" (see page 25), and then use a fork to seal the edges.

4. To fry the pies, heat the oil in a heavy pot over medium-high heat, stirring occasionally until it reaches 375 degrees. Gently lower the dumplings into the oil, using a slotted spoon or wire basket. Cook for about 3 minutes or until the pies are golden brown. Remove from the oil using the same utensil you used to put them in. Drain on paper towels before serving warm.

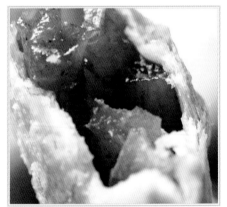

Quebecois Apple Dumplings with Mincemeat and Cheddar

Quebecois Apple Dumplings with Mincemeat and Cheddar

Makes 4 dumplings

Every time I look into apple dumplings or Quebecois food, this intensely English recipe—complete with cheddar cheese, rum, and mincemeat—seems to turn up. It's a delicious dish, but I suspect that it didn't make it to Quebec via France.

FILLING

1/2 cup shredded cheddar cheese

1/2 cup mincemeat (see note)

1/4 cup rum

1/4 cup brown sugar

2 tablespoons butter, at room temperature

4 apples, peeled and cored

1/2 cup heavy cream

2 tablespoons sugar

2 teaspoons lemon zest

NOTE: Not ground meat! Look for it in a jar on the baking shelf of your super-market.

WRAPPERS

"North American Pie and Dumpling Wrappers," page 258

Oil for cookie sheet

1. Preheat your oven to 375 degrees.

2. To make the filling, combine the cheese, mincemeat, rum, brown sugar, and butter in a medium bowl, and mix until the ingredients are well combined and evenly distributed.

3. Stand 1 peeled and cored apple in the center of a wrapper square, and fill the center cavity with one-quarter of the cheese-spice mixture. Lift the opposite corners of the dough square and bring them together. Now pinch the edges to form sealed seams.

4. Mix the cream, sugar, and lemon zest into a thick paste, and brush over the top of each dumpling.

5. Place the dumplings on a well-oiled cookie sheet and bake for 1 hour or until the crust is golden brown. Don't overbake or the glaze will burn. Serve warm as is or with cream, whipped cream, and/or ice cream.

The Perfect Piecrust Contains. . .

Lots of people like to talk pie and for most of them, their favorite subtopic is the crust. They may use all sorts of fats—shortening, butter, margarine, or even oils—but when the arguments die down and the discussion tapers off to whispers, everybody agrees that the ultimate fat for piecrust is lard.

Lard? Does it even exist anymore?

I knew that highly processed blocks and tubs of lard were sold in local stores, but a look at how it was produced immediately turned me off. If I was going to try the stuff, it was going to have to be something a bit better.

Connoisseurs of lard—and surprisingly there are lots of them—tell us that the "proper" lard is called "leaf lard" or "neutral lard." It's found around the pig's kidneys and abdomen. I imagined myself searching for months to find this, but before I even began, I spotted it in the freezer case of a local Chinese supermarket.

To render it out, all you need to do is chop it in 1-inch squares, and heat it in a pot over low heat. Continue cooking, occasionally stirring, until the solids begin to brown; like caramelizing onions, it takes a couple of hours and can't be rushed. Then strain out the remaining liquid, and refrigerate it in a container with a lid that closes tightly.

While the remaining brown stuff isn't called for in any recipe here, it's used extensively in the Deep South, where it's known as "cracklings." Save it in the refrigerator if you cook dishes from that region.

Hard-to-Find Ingredients

Most—but not all—of the ingredients in this book can be found in typical American

supermarkets. Others will need a bit more searching out. I encourage you to begin at local

ethnic groceries—visiting them can be a real adventure. In addition, the neighborhoods

they're located in often have snack shops, bakeries, or restaurants that give you a chance to

taste the recipes—or at least their commercial versions.

If you live in an urban area or large university town, there could well be the

perfect market waiting for you with all the ingredients you'll be searching for.

So . . . what are these items?

Aleppo Pepper Sometimes known as halaby pepper, it's a red chili with medium heat that comes from the Middle East. It's often the heat you taste in Turkish cuisine, so their groceries will stock it, and specialty spice shops will, too.

Amaretti Cookies The name means "little, bitter things." They're really traditionally sweet, crunchy Italian cookies that are as much an ingredient as a snack. In stores, try to avoid the ones packed in beautifully decorated gift tins; they cost a fortune and leave you with a really fancy-looking empty can at the end. They'll be much cheaper in shops that cater to Italian expats.

Amchur Powder Dried and ground sour mango. It's used as a flavoring all over South Asia. Find it in Indian markets.

Sweet Azuki Bean Paste/Sweet Red Bean Paste An almost always canned sweetened bean product that's used as a filling in Asian desserts. Easy to find in Japanese shops and fairly common in other Asian groceries. Getting it on the Internet is a challenge unless you search under the Japanese name "Yude Azuki."

Black Sesame Seeds From a tropical plant, they're commonly used in Asian cuisines. Korean and Japanese stores stock them in large bags.

Chinese Black Vinegar Made from rice and malt, this vinegar is used as a seasoning and sauce ingredient. It's a staple item in Chinese groceries and can sometimes be found in the Asian section of regular supermarkets.

Chinese Rice Wine A fermented rice product used for seasoning. Like black vinegar above, it can be found in any Chinese food store.

Chinese Ham Very similar to American dry-cured "country hams." In many Chinese butchers and meat departments in the United States, both are sold side by side. Substitute country ham if you can't get Chinese.

Chipotle Peppers Smoked jalapeño peppers often packed in a delicious adobo sauce. You used to have to go to Mexican groceries to buy them, but nowadays they often show up in supermarkets. Since you'll almost never use a whole can, freeze the remaining peppers and sauce for future use.

Exotic Mushrooms These include oyster

and porcini and are available fresh in high-end produce shops and in dried form at ethnic grocers. Polish stores often have a great selection of dried mushrooms. On the Web, there's a whole universe of mushroom vendors and sites.

Fennel Seeds Fennel is a classic part of both the Indian and Italian flavor palettes. Buy the seeds from Indian groceries.

Fenugreek Seeds and/or Leaves Known as "methi" in Indian cuisine and used extensively there, you can find these at Indian shops, where the seeds will often be in plastic bags and the leaves in boxes.

Fish Sauce, or Nam Pla A liquid from fermented and salted fish, it's a key flavor in many Southeast Asian foods. Although considered strange not long ago, fish sauce is finding its way to supermarket shelves and is a staple at Asian groceries.

Fontina/Fontal Cheese Not the one from Denmark but rather a cheese from the far north of Italy. Those labeled "Fontina D.O.P." are from the Aosta Valley and most expensive. Generally they're found in specialty cheese shops. "Fontal" is from the neighboring

Piedmont region and is often found in better supermarket cheese departments. For the recipes in this book, Fontal and Italian Fontina are interchangeable.

Garam Masala Powder A classic Indian spice mixture. Try the supermarket first, but it's a staple at Indian groceries. Don't confuse with "Whole Garam Marsala."

Gorgonzola Cheese The Italian blue cheese, it's often in supermarkets and usually in specialty shops. In a pinch, substitute other blue cheese varieties.

Ground Asafetida A Middle Eastern spice used often in Indian cooking, it's the dried, powdered gum of the asafetida plant and is sold in tiny plastic containers. Beware: It has a strange odor when it's raw and doesn't take on its "real" flavor until cooked. Buy it in Indian markets where it can also be called "hing" or "heeng."

Ground Chilies in Oil Used in China as both a seasoning and a hot sauce. If your supermarket has a section with jars of Chinese seasonings, it could well be there; otherwise, any Chinese grocery will have it.

Hearts of Palm The shoots of the cabbage palm, peeled and canned. While in some places it's cultivated for food, it's also harvested wild in the Amazon rainforest. Buy it at Latin American groceries.

Hoisin Sauce Another of those Chinese sauces that's sneaking onto American supermarket shelves. If you don't find it there, it's a staple at Asian groceries.

Jamaican Curry Powder A bit different—and hotter—than Indian curry powders, it gives Island foods their distinctive flavor. Caribbean groceries stock it, and Latin ones often have it, too.

Kimchi The legendary preserved food of Korea (see "Just What Is Kimchi?" on page 44). Try to buy this from a Korean grocery or Web site. Versions sold elsewhere might be diluted for "foreign palates" and will lack the requisite zing.

Mango or Tamarind Chutney A condiment that can be thought of as India's "salsa." Most Indian groceries have a large section of prepared chutneys, and some might sneak their way into your local supermarket.

Mustard Oil Pressed from mustards seeds, this oil is used all over Asia as a food, massage oil, and medicine. It can be found in most Indian and many Chinese markets; indeed, it can even be found on eBay.

Palm Sugar blocks of sugar produced from a type of palm tree using a method that's similar to maple sugar. Thai and Indian groceries usually carry it.

Pancetta Italian preserved pork belly. Not exactly bacon—because it isn't smoked—but considered both a cold cut and a cooking ingredient in that cuisine. Your best choice for buying it is the deli counter of better stores, but it's also available presliced and packed in plastic in many supermarkets.

Pine Nuts/Pignoli Edible pine-tree seeds. They're commonly used in Italian and Middle Eastern cooking and show up in Asian and Native American dishes, too. Look for them at Arabic markets, where the price can be a bit more reasonable than your local supermarket (although they're never cheap).

Rice Paper Spring Roll Wrappers The premade wrappers for "Shrimp and Cucumber

Spring Rolls" (see page 74) can be found at Vietnamese groceries, where they're considered a staple food, and at larger Asian supermarkets.

Roasted Kasha Roasted, hulled buckwheat. Long a staple in Eastern European Jewish cooking, it is found in the kosher section of the supermarket. Otherwise, look in kosher groceries, delis, or (believe it or not) health-food stores that stock a wide variety of grains.

Semolina Flour High-gluten flour for pasta and breads. Sometimes it shows up on super-market shelves, but you're more likely to find it at an Italian specialty shop or a health-food store that has a wide selection of bulk grains.

Sesame Oil Oil pressed from sesame seeds. Buy it at any Asian store—and don't worry, it lasts a really long time.

Shiitake Mushrooms Also known as "Chinese black mushrooms," they've been cultivated in Asia for at least a thousand years and are sold in fresh and dried form in Asian shops and specialty produce stores. Shiitake cultivation is becoming popular enough for them to sometimes show up fresh in local farmers markets.

Sichuan Peppercorns These offer the famous "numbing" flavor that's distinctive in that region's cooking. Illegal in the U.S. for many years, they're now sold in Chinese groceries.

Sumac Powder This dark-red spice provides the distinct acidic fruity taste of Middle Eastern dishes. Find it in Turkish, Middle Eastern, and specialty spice shops.

Thai Curry Paste Not to be confused with any other curry paste or powder, it's another one of those stealth supermarket items. It's sold in cans and recloseable plastic tubs and is easiest to find at big Asian stores, but if you're lucky enough to have a Thai specialty store in your neighborhood, try it first.

Water Chestnuts The seed of an aquatic plant that looks just a bit like a chestnut, they're available canned in most Asian groceries.

Whole Black Mustard Seeds The raw material for the stuff you put on hot dogs and also an important spice in a wide variety of cuisines. Most easily purchased at Indian markets.

And If You Can't Find Them Locally?

Almost every item in this glossary can be found at big Internet food sites. You probably know them already, but here they are for reference.

www.amazon.com

www.bulkfoods.com

www.gourmetstore.com

www.igourmet.com

www.penzeys.com

www.savoryspiceshop.com

HARD-TO-FIND INGREDIENTS

Just as with retail stores, there are also specialized Web sites that have remarkable variety. For the most part, they are catering to homesick expats and offer all sorts of interesting surprises. While it would be impossible to catalog all of them, here's a tiny—and random—selection to get you started.

Popular Asian items: www.asianfoodgrocer.com

A wide variety of grains: www.bobsredmill.com

Caribbean foods: www.caribcon.com

Cheeses and cheese-making supplies: www.cheesesupply.com

Italian groceries, fancy foods, and gifts: www.ditalia.com

Complete selection of Thai foods: www.importfood.com

Mushroom specialists: www.jrmushroomsandspecialties.com

Korean and Japanese products, including a whole section devoted to kimchi: www.koamart.com

Comprehensive selection of Mexican products: www.mexgrocer.com

Everything Turkish: www.tulumba.com

INDEX